WALKING IN
SUNSHINE

WALKING IN
SUNSHINE

A fully illustrated comprehensive guide to airbrush
and HVLP Spray Tanning.
Packed with crucial information for qualified spray tanning
technicians and anyone interested in making a career in
spray tanning.

Samantha Whitehead

www.castlepointtanning.co.uk

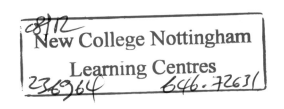

New College Nottingham
Learning Centres
236964   646.7263/

First Published 2010
This Edition published 2011
By Samantha Whitehead

ISBN: 978-0-9568959-0-5

Contents

Introduction

Back in the '50s and '60s, the only tanning products that people bought were oils and calamine lotion. Things were pretty simple in those days: you sat in the sun for hours at a time, covered in cooking oil. You burnt yourself to a crisp and then slapped on copious quantities of cooling white lotion to take away the pain. Next you shed your skin like a snake and repeated the process the following year, on the one or two occasional sunny days that came our way.

That was pretty much it. Then in the '70s and '80s, tanning started to develop into a vast industry of sunscreens, moisturising lotions, artificial tanning creams, sunbeds and of course, holidays in the sun.

Two weeks on the Med or the Costa Brava was what we craved and the objective was very simple: get brown, in most cases by dangerously burning ourselves.

Gradually we became aware that too much sun on fair skin was no good to us and we reluctantly came to accept that protection, in the form of high factor sun creams and moisturising creams, was necessary for safe sunbathing. Risks to health and long-term damage to the skin took the fun out of the sun for all but the most obstinate and so alternatives had to be found.

Modern tanning beds became a preferred choice for many and with them came the realisation that a suntan need not be an annual event, but could be sustained throughout the year. We could even top up on a daily basis if we wanted to.

Undoubtedly a suntan makes you feel thinner, healthier and more attractive and the beauty industry rapidly geared up to meet our demands.

But recent studies prove that prolonged exposure to ultraviolet light, whether from the sun or tanning beds, can be a cause of skin cancer. So there's still the need to find a way of tanning that doesn't age the skin, and more importantly still, isn't carcinogenic.

Rumours are now circulating that sunbed users will soon be issued with cards limiting sunbed usage - good news for the tanning technician. Sunbed Regulations Act 2010 came in to force; 8 April 2011- see Health and Safety page 159.

Men seem to have a higher risk of skin cancer and that suggests a reluctance to use sun creams while sunbathing or working outside. Men also feel a little embarrassed booking a personal spray tan application, but the numbers taking the plunge are on the increase. The booth option for men at present remains the favourite method.

Finally, there's the development of the self-tanning creams and compounds in which all health risks were virtually eliminated and an instant, albeit relatively short-lived, tan was quickly achieved. Any part of the body could be tanned at any time, but the downside was that the result was often streaky, imperfect and rather orange. People's hands also became very orange through applying the creams. A tanning cream tan typically only lasted two to three days, so a lasting tan required a certain amount of dedication.

We can reasonably conclude that whatever the dangers and difficulties, tanning is here to stay and there will always be a market for new systems that do a decent job safely, efficiently and at a reasonable price.

Airbrush spray tan does all three, but with **one** significant advantage over the other systems - a seamless, precise, perfect and even tan. It's as complete and streak-free as a tan can be and most important of all, it is **not** harmful.

1

How does spray tanning work?

There are two principal factors which need to be explained and understood.

Firstly the chemistry of the lotion itself and then the equipment which delivers the solution: a separate airbrush gun and separate compressor.

The chemistry

The first thing to remember is that an airbrush spray tan does not paint the body brown. The solution is not paint, or even a stain. The active ingredient is DHA (Dihydroxyacetone), which reacts with the amino acids in the epidermis; the uppermost layer of our skin, which we shed daily. The DHA starts to work within about two hours of the tan application and carries on for a further twelve hours.

This is known as the Maillard reaction, and it's the same as the browning that occurs when an apple has been sliced and allowed to stand.

DHA has been used cosmetically for over 30 years without any harmful effects being reported, and it's the active ingredient in all brands of self-tanning creams, sprays and foams.

Airbrush spray tanning solution or lotion has the added advantage of containing a bronzing agent, so the technician can see where she/he has sprayed, and can achieve perfect all-over coverage. Of course if the skin is already slightly tanned then it's a little harder to tell which areas of skin have been treated.

A skilled operator will quickly learn, however, that a methodical approach to spraying gives a much better chance of perfect coverage, with or without the bronzing agent. Let's not forget that the bronzing agent also has the added benefit that it gives your client something immediate to show. That said, it's very important that you explain to your client that this immediate tanned appearance is just the bronzing agent and will mostly wash off upon showering, leaving the true tan underneath.

The spray tan solution needs to stay on the skin for approximately 12 hours before bathing – overnight is ideal. Remind clients not to sit on leather upholstery before showering; it's skin, even if it's not still attached to the animal, and will be affected by the solution. Always sit on a towel. Many people worry about the coloured water that runs off them when they have their first shower, so be sure to let clients know that this is inevitable and of course won't affect their end result.

Depending on the skin type, an airbrush tan can last for anything up to ten days. It can be maintained for as long as you need it, with top-up applications of tanning solutions applied up to six days after the first application.

The colour you get from a spray tan won't wash off, but it will start to fade as the upper layers of the epidermis wear away naturally. If your client isn't pleased with the results from your spray tan, remind them that they can always try to speed the fading process by soaking in a hot bath and gently exfoliating with a washcloth or loofah. Using baby oil in the bath will also help and soaking for ten minutes before exfoliation will help loosen the dead skin cells. As a rule, it will take around a week for the spray tan to disappear totally.

Understanding the skin

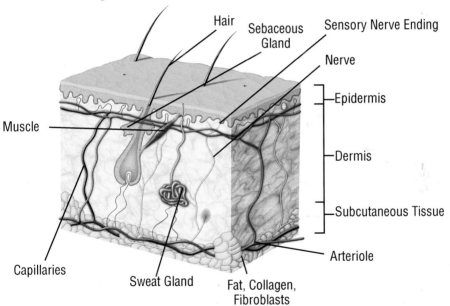

The skin consists of three layers. Spray tanning concentrates on the epidermis.

1. The epidermis
2. The dermis
3. The hyperdermis, also known as subcutis

The epidermis is the outer layer of the skin where tanning takes place. It's made up of layers that we naturally shed daily, and is classed as a dead layer of skin, containing no blood vessels or nerves. There are two main layers: the horny layer (stratum corneum) and the germinal or basal layer.

The horny layer (shown as the lighter pink top layer) is the outermost layer of the epidermis and the one most affected by tanning products.

The epidermis generally regenerates a new layer of skin every six weeks and the daily shedding is normally helped with washing, drying, exfoliating, usage of cosmetic products and cleaning materials such as loofahs.

The skin's absorption

Chemicals can be absorbed via:

1. Sweat glands, through which water-soluble chemicals can pass

2. Tiny channels between the layers of the epidermis, through which water soluble chemicals can pass

3. Hair follicles, through which oil soluble products can pass.

The rate of absorption varies depending on:

1. The concentration of the chemical

2. The duration of time the chemical is on the skin

3. Where the chemical is applied, as different parts of the body absorb at different rates

4. The condition of the skin.

Having a real understanding of the skin will help the tanning technician to provide good before and aftercare information for their clients to get the best spray tan possible.

Selecting a suitable DHA percentage

A good rule to follow is to select a spray tanning colour tone based on the natural colour of the skin.

The most common spray tan tone percentages are 8%, 10% and 12%.

Some fair-skinned clients may not want their result from a spray tan to be dark and of course a darker tan tone percentage may not look natural on them. If this is the case it would be best to spray with a lighter DHA percentage, probably 8%. A client who has a slight colour to their natural skin would look best with a medium tan tone percentage, probably 10%. A client with a naturally darker skin would be best suited to a 12% tan tone. You really do need to discuss what end result the client requires and know the product you're using very well.

You should keep in mind too that if you use a DHA with a percentage that's too high for a client's natural skin tone, they might end up with a tan that will wear off in a noticeably uneven and patchy way. Applying too much DHA to a fair-skinned person can look orange after a couple of days. The pH levels in skin can be different after exfoliation and this can cause orange undertones. These can however be minimised by using a pH balancing soap before the spray tan.

It's better to be safe and spray tan a lighter percentage of DHA to your client's skin if you're not certain.

There are many tan tone percentages on the market today, ranging from 6% right through to 16%, and knowing your product and the result it gives for most skin types, will only come after lots of experience.

It is essential to nourish and hydrate your skin in order to maintain the life of your spray tan, so selecting a solution with ingredients that promote those processes will benefit the tan. If the tanning solution is high in alcohol content, it can dry and irritate the skin. The higher the DHA in the spray tanning solution, the likelier it is to contain a higher alcohol preservative.

You can ask the manufacturer of your spray tanning solution for a material safety data sheet (MSDS), which will explain all the ingredients of the tanning solution. In most countries and states it is recommended that you have an MSDS for each individual product available at all times.

If your client has a special event coming up, and they've never had a spray tan, perform a patch test and ask the client to leave the spray tan solution on their skin for 24 hours. I'd recommend using the underside of the arm or an area of the body that's out of sight.

If the patch test was successful and no reaction was found you might want to recommend the client comes in for a trial spray tan at least four weeks before their event.

This allows enough time for:

- The spray tan to wear off and lets you and the client decide if the tone percentage was right

- Testing alternative percentage levels if required

- Judging on which day the tan looked best, so you can time the full session to perfection.

It also makes the client comfortable with you as the technician, the surroundings and the process itself.

Material safety data sheets

Material safety data sheets (MSDS) provide detailed information on specific chemicals and chemical mixtures. The manufacturers of the various spray tanning solutions should produce material safety data sheets for each individual product, which will usually include instructions for their safe use, describe any potential hazards, and list all ingredients.

Even when the tanning solution contains no hazardous ingredients, it may contain ingredients to which a client could be allergic; some contain nut extract such as Juglans regia (walnut), which could of course be extremely dangerous to a client with a severe nut allergy.

One sure-fire way of testing the quality of your solutions supplier is to ask for any relevant data sheets. A good, reputable company will provide them. I've heard plenty of accounts of product distributors failing to supply the appropriate data sheets, and even denying any need for them. I've even come across a provider myself who didn't know what they are...and after my explanation declared that there was no need to supply one.

The reality is that both operatives and clients need to be aware of the potential side effects of any tanning product. A closer inspection of material safety data sheets may even raise concerns about respiratory problems; manufacturers will usually recommend that any asthma sufferers consult their doctor before using spray products.

It's your duty as a spray tan technician to ensure the welfare of your clients wherever possible, so if your supplier is unhelpful, find a new one. Go directly to the product manufacturer if you're encountering difficulties.

Quite apart from it being a moral responsibility, providing the information found within an MSDS can also protect your financial welfare; a client suffering an adverse reaction to your spray tan may well result in a lawsuit or insurance claim against your business.

Storing your tanning solution

You do need to care for your spray tanning solutions. Storage is very important for keeping your solutions in tip-top condition; in return you'll get the correct spray tan results for that product. If storage recommendations don't appear on the bottle, ask the manufacturer for this information (usually contained in the MSDS). If the product is mishandled or stored incorrectly, the performance and stability of the solution can be affected.

Most spray tanning solutions need to be stored in a cool, dry place, out of direct sunlight. The best storage place after opening is a refrigerator. This will achieve the maximum lifespan, but care should be taken so the solution doesn't freeze. Alternatively you could store in a cool cupboard.

Exposure to heat, air and light can cause its shelf life to lessen and this can affect the DHA's performance, so make sure the cap is replaced immediately and securely after use.

Shelf life is approximately six months, after which the tanning action of DHA slowly loses its effectiveness. It can be up to a year if the solution is stored correctly and unopened. You may find it helpful to mark each bottle with the date of purchase.

Do not mix old solutions with new solutions, as this will just weaken the new solution. You should never mix solutions from different manufacturers; you do not know how it will perform. Always gently shake your solution before you use it, to remix all the ingredients.

Sunscreens

It's important to understand that spray tanning solutions contain no sunscreen or sun block of any kind and the reasons for this are quite straightforward.

Firstly, sunscreens or sun blocks need to be applied regularly: every two to three hours when sitting for lengthy periods in the hot summer sun. Factor 25 or more is recommended for the first few days, particularly for very pale skins.

If sunscreens **were** included within the spray tanning solution, it would only be in tiny amounts...the spray tanning solutions would have to be applied onto the skin regularly and in large amounts to provide any protection at all from the harmful sun while sunbathing. What's more, such large quantities would turn the skin a most unattractive and unacceptable shade of orange.

Simply put, you couldn't get a decent tanned effect if spray tanning solutions contained adequate sunscreen.

So it's vital that you make it clear to your clients that a spray tan does not contain any sunscreen and they must still protect themselves when going in the sun, or they will burn.

Some clients are shocked to learn this, mainly because it's easy to forget that the brown skin they've achieved is not permanent. It's worth noting that clients should not apply a sunscreen containing oil as this will prematurely wear their spray tan away. I always recommend a non-oily sunscreen.

How does spray tanning work?

2
The equipment

An airbrush gun is designed to deliver liquids mixed with air as a fine spray or mist. Traditionally artists have used airbrushes to deliver paint to paper. In our case we are delivering a fine spray of tanning solution to the skin.

The main characteristic of the airbrush effect is that it leaves absolutely no brush marks or texture on the surface whatsoever, just a perfectly even and extremely thin coating of colour.

The perfection of this application will come with good training and plenty of practice.

The airbrush gun is perfect for spraying an instant tan onto the skin for the result is as seamless and flawless as the skin itself. This is rarely achieved when applying tanning creams by hand, where the result can often be streaky, patchy and very orange.

An airbrush gun is powered by compressed air, which is generated, as you might expect, by a compressor.

The compressor draws air in from the atmosphere, takes out the moisture and delivers it under pressure to the airbrush, where small amounts of solution are picked up as the air travels through. The air and solution are then forced out through a tiny nozzle at the end of the airbrush as a fine spray or mist.

Modern compressors are small, very quiet and robust, for the most part requiring no significant maintenance or servicing.

Imported, cheaper spray tanning equipment is often made for infrequent, light use, and is normally quite unsuitable for sustained salon work. They'll burn out very quickly, meaning you'll have to let them cool down between sessions, or at worst, replace them entirely. These cheaper imported models may be ok if you intend to spray tan yourself at home once a week, but they're a false economy for the professional tanning technician.

We also need to make sure we are buying genuine products and not imitations, so make sure you buy from reputable suppliers. Please bear in mind when looking for your equipment, VAT and postage may not already be included in the listed price.

I've included various photographs to give you a visual guide to spray tanning equipment. All pictures used, except the Microclene extractor unit, are from the Iwata range, which I've chosen as it has a fantastic track record of producing high quality products that last. I'm a registered reseller for Iwata and Microclene, so do take note that I have a vested interest. That said, the whole reason I became a reseller was because I've spent years using and testing their products, took the time and trouble to visit the workshops and meet the people involved, and have complete faith in both the products and the companies involved.

Airbrush guns

There are two main types of airbrush guns for spray tanning: the dual action airbrush gun and the single action airbrush gun. Both are designed for precision airbrush spray tanning work. These airbrush guns should have bottom feed pots, meaning that your tanning solution pot attaches beneath the gun rather than above.

Both single and dual airbrush applications take around 15-20 minutes to apply.

Single action airbrush gun

A single action airbrush is great for beginners as well as experienced technicians, being an internal-mix type. This requires just the press-down action on the airbrush gun, for air and product, which is much easier to control. The solution adjustment knob allows you to preset the amount of product to allow through the airbrush gun.

For the more experienced technician who wants to apply a spray tan at different application levels, maybe for sculpting or defining, partial tanning to match a natural suntan on a client, or lighter application on very dry areas of the skin for instance, the single action airbrush can be rather fiddly, since you'll have to keep changing the presetting knob on the gun, during the one session.

The Iwata Revolution SAR features:

- Suction-feed

- Single-action

- Internal-mix

- Adjustment knob on handle to preset product flow

- Larger 0.5mm nozzle suitable for thicker or heavier paints

- Fine detail to 1.5" (0.5mm to 38mm) spray pattern with the one size nozzle

- Ergonomic handle design

- Ten year warranty.

Dual action airbrush gun

With the dual action gun you can vary the amount of product being sprayed by moving the trigger back and forth; there's no need to preset the airbrush. Most of the time while spray tanning, you'll have the trigger all the way back, but you may need a lighter application for certain areas of a client's body.

As with the single action, there's a button on top of the airbrush gun. Here it's pushed down for airflow and pulled back for the solution. It allows a controlled application with hardly any product waste or overspray.

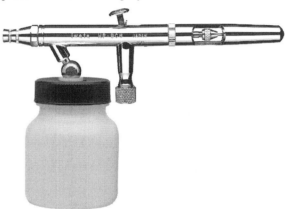

The Iwata Eclipse BCS features:

- Suction-feed

- Dual-action

- Internal-mix

- 0.5mm needle and nozzle

- Fine detail to 2" (0.5mm to 50mm) spray pattern

- Drop-in, self-centring nozzle for perfect alignment and ease of assembly

- Ten year warranty

- The Eclipse BCS has the option to change to a 0.35mm needle, nozzle and nozzle cap for even finer detail.

The pressure gauge on compressors for both single and dual action airbrush guns should be set at around 10-12psi. Always take the pressure reading while the airbrush gun is spraying and then set to the required psi level. This rule applies to most compressors and separate airbrush gun systems.

LVLP

A Low Volume High Pressure (LVHP) gun works in a similar way to the precision airbrush gun as the product can be controlled. Application time is around 7-10 minutes. If speed of application is a priority, perhaps when holding a salon or tanning party, then this gun could be for you. It will produce more overspray than the single and dual airbrush guns, but not as much as most HVLP guns.

The Iwata Eclipse G6

The Eclipse G6 is a unique 'pistol-grip' airbrush. It looks like a small spray gun, but performs like a large airbrush. It has a special fitting which allows use of suction-feed bottles as well as gravity feed cups. This gun has the option of controlling your spray tan application in a circular or fan pattern.

The fan pattern seems to be more popular for spray tanning, as there's less chance of causing banding/striping with a fast application on the skin, like *some* HVLP systems can produce.

The circular pattern can be used for very fine application and coverage can be as little as 1mm by using the adjustment knob on the gun, while the fan pattern has the ability to cover up to 80mm if needed. You would need a stronger compressor (the Iwata Power Jet HT compressor is recommended) to run this airbrush gun and the pressure on the gauge should be set slightly higher, at 12-20psi.

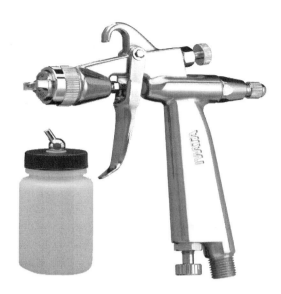

The Eclipse G6 features:

- Suction-feed and gravity-feed

- 0.6mm stainless-steel nozzle

- Dual-purpose air cap and fan adjustment valve for round pattern and oval/fan pattern

- Long tapered needle for smooth transition between fine and wide spray

- 1mm to 80mm spray pattern

- 10 year warranty.

HVLP

There are so many high volume low pressure (HVLP) systems that I'd be here all day just trying to list them.

HVLP systems do offer the advantage of a speedy application, making them well suited to a busy salon offering continuous spray tanning. The downside of this can be the excess solution used during each application.

Many technicians I've spoken with have stated that although originally taught HVLP, they later qualified in precision airbrush spray tanning, so as to cater for both applications.

Precision airbrushing spray tanning is the slowest method, taking 15-20 minutes to apply, LVLP 7-10 minutes and HVLP around 5 minutes.

Precision is more adaptable, so it does have its advantages.

You can use the same system of single action and dual-action airbrush gun with separate compressor for other services offered to your clients, by changing the needle and pot for some of the following:

- Airbrush makeup

- Airbrush tattooing

- Airbrush nail art

- Airbrush hair art

- Airbrush face painting.

Less overspray is produced and less solution used, so you'll find your profits per application are higher.

Some HVLP systems are difficult to transport in your technician's trolley, depending on the trolley type; they also tend to be noisier and some blow out cold air.

The precision airbrush guns have been around for many years, suggesting longevity of life. A good make will last well, and there are plenty of suppliers should parts need to be replaced.

As for which system is the best, it's a tricky one to call – each machine has its advantages, but in the final analysis it's up to the technician to decide which system is better for their clients, and which would best complement their business.

Compressors

First of all, you need to decide what you want your compressor for. A busy salon will need a good, large compressor that will hold up to many spray tans being performed one after another, whereas a mobile technician won't need such a big compressor and also needs to think about its weight and ease of transportation.

A fundamental point to which you should give serious consideration is your business plan. If you're opening a new salon it would be sensible to go for the larger compressor from the start, if you can afford it. After all, if things go well you may be extremely busy, and a burnt-out small compressor that wasn't up to the job is the kind of additional cost and inconvenience you don't need.

Mobile technicians' compressors get a cool-down period between spray tans because of travelling and set-up times, so a smaller compressor might be the most suitable option.

One important point to remember, with both salon and mobile usage, is that using excessive pressure will release too much spray into the immediate atmosphere, making breathing uncomfortable for both technician and client and potentially damaging your equipment.

If a compressor is going to be used for **spray tanning** you should get it serviced once a year to keep it running at optimum performance. Experience tells us that many technicians are using compressors at too high a pressure setting and without adequate ventilation. This causes the tanning solution to get drawn into the compressor, clogging the filter and motor and potentially causing irreparable damage.

The compressor should be situated in a source of clean, dry air, as far away as possible from the direction that you are spraying in, and wiped over with a damp cloth at the end of the day. Compressors damaged by drawn-in overspray are seen as being misused and won't be covered by a warranty.

There are many compressors on the market; here's a quick guide from the Iwata range so you can compare and choose the right model for your own usage.

The Sprint Jet

Iwata Studio Series compressors are powerful, compact and quiet. With oil-less piston motors, they are low maintenance and affordably priced. This compressor is more suitable for the mobile technician or low usage in a salon.

The Iwata Sprint Jet features:

- Low maintenance, oil-less single piston air compressor

- Quiet-running 1/8 HP induction motor

- Air flow at 0psi: 0.42 CFM (12 lpm)

- Working pressure from 0psi to 35psi

- Coiled vinyl cooling hose and filter, which removes moisture and prevents pulsing

- Pressure gauge

- Adjustable bleed valve on the bottom of the filter bowl to regulate air pressure

- Comes with a 3-metre (10') vinyl hose and adapters to fit most airbrushes

- 1/4 BSP outlet on moisture filter (1/8 outlet on compressor connects via cooling hose to 1/8 inlet on filter)

- Size: 25 x 18 x 16cm

- Weight: 4kg

- Voltage: 220-240V 50Hz

- Noise level: 50 decibels

- Duty cycle: 40 minutes' use. Allow the motor to rest for at least 20 minutes after each cycle of use

- One year warranty.

The Sprint Jet has a manual on/off switch. It's light, very portable and suitable for either occasional or professional use.

The Smart Jet Pro

Smart Technology automatically turns the compressor on when you press your airbrush trigger, providing instant air at the pressure set, and turns off again when the airbrush is not in use. The Smart Jet Pro has a metal protective case with integral regulator and pressure gauge. This compressor is suitable for mobile and salon use and can perform many continuous spray tans.

The Iwata Smart Jet Pro features:

- Low maintenance, oil-less single piston air compressor

- Quiet-running 1/8 HP induction motor

- Air flow: 0.42 CFM (12 lpm)

- Working pressure from 0psi to 35psi

- Smart Technology automatic switching reduces running time and motor wear (30psi on / 50psi off)

- Protective outer case

- Cooling hose and filter inside case, which remove the moisture and prevent pulsing

- Mounted pressure gauge

- Air regulator for precise air pressure adjustment

- Comes with a 3-metre (10') vinyl hose

- One 1/4 BSP outlet

- Built-in airbrush holder

- Size: 26.5 x 31 x 15.5cm

- Weight: 6.3kg

- Voltage: 220-240V 50Hz

- Noise level: 50 decibels

- Duty cycle: 60 minutes' use. Allow the motor to rest for at least 20 minutes after each use

- One year warranty.

The Power Jet Lite

The Power Jet Lite is twice as powerful as a Sprint Jet, so you can run two fine airbrushes or one high-flow airbrush or a small spray gun.

Smart Technology automatically turns the compressor on when the airbrush trigger is pressed, and turns it off again when the airbrush is not in use. The Power Jet Lite has a metal protective case with integral regulator and pressure gauge.

The Iwata Power Jet Lite features:

- Low maintenance, oil-less twin piston air compressor

- Quiet-running 1/6 HP induction motor

- Air flow at 0psi: 0.88 CFM (25 lpm)

- Working pressure: 0psi to 60psi

- Smart Technology automatic switching reduces running time and motor wear (40psi on / 60psi off)

- Protective outer case

- Moisture filter inside case, which removes the moisture and prevent pulsing

- Mounted pressure gauge

- Air regulator for precise air pressure adjustment

- One 1/4 BSP outlet

- Comes with a 3-metre (10') vinyl hose

- Built-in airbrush holder

- Size: 26.5 x 31 x 15.5cm

- Weight: 7.9kg

- Voltage: 220-240V 50Hz

- Noise level: 52 decibels

- Duty cycle: 60 minutes' use. Please allow the motor to rest for at least 20 minutes after each cycle

- One year warranty.

The Power Jet Pro

The Power Jet Pro is twice as powerful as a Sprint Jet, so you can run two fine airbrushes or one high-flow airbrush or a small spray gun. It has dual air regulators and gauges for setting the pressure for each airbrush independently.

The Power Jet Pro has a two-litre tank reservoir, which increases moisture separation and smoothes out the airflow. This type of machine is better for when heavy use is expected or higher pressures required.

The Power Jet Pro features:

- Low maintenance, oil-less twin piston air compressor

- Quiet-running 1/6 HP induction motor

- 2-litre storage tank

- Air flow at 0psi: 0.88 CFM (25 lpm)

- Working pressure from 0psi to 60psi

- Dual moisture filters

- Dual mounted pressure gauges

- Dual air regulators for precise pressure adjustment

- Dual quick disconnect ports (2 x 1/4 BSP outlets with 2 x 1/4 BSP quick releases)

- Dual airbrush holders

- Smart Technology automatic switching reduces running time and motor wear (40psi on / 60psi off)

- Protective outer case

- Comes with two 3m (10') coiled vinyl hoses

- Size: 26.5 x 31 x 15.5cm

- Weight: 11.9kg

- Voltage: 220-240V 50Hz

- Noise level: 52 decibels

- Duty cycle: 60 minutes' use. Make sure you let the motor rest for at least 20 minutes after each cycle of use

- One year warranty.

The Smart Jet Plus HT

The Smart Jet Plus HT is nearly twice as powerful as a Sprint or Smart Jet, so you can run two fine airbrushes or one high-flow airbrush or a small spray gun (round pattern only).

Once again, Smart Technology automatically takes care of turning the machine on and off. The Smart Jet Plus HT has a reservoir in its handle (hence HT – handle tank), and a detachable regulator.

The Iwata Smart Jet Plus HT features:

- Low maintenance, oil-less single piston air compressor

- Quiet-running 1/6 HP motor (54dB)

- Smart Technology automatic switching reduces running time and motor wear

- 450cc reservoir built into the handle, smoothes the airflow and cools the air

- Pressure gauge

- Detachable air regulator for precise air pressure adjustment

- Working pressure from 1psi to 60psi

- Comes with a 3-metre (10') vinyl hose

- Built-in airbrush holder

- Size: 28 x 16 x 27.5cm

- Weight: 5.5kg

- Air flow: 0.81 CFM (23 lpm)

- Voltage: 220-240V 50Hz

- One year warranty

The Power Jet Plus HT

The Power Jet Plus HT is twice as powerful as The smart Jet Plus HT and nearly twice the power of the Power Jet Lite, so it can run a number of airbrushes or a small spray gun of 0.7 – 0.8mm nozzle size with fan pattern application. Alternatively, it's got enough power to run the Iwata Eclipse G6 gun.

The Iwata Power Jet Plus HT features:

- Low maintenance, oil-less twin piston air compressor

- Quiet-running 1/4 HP motor (56 - 58dB)

- Smart Technology automatic switching reduces running time and motor wear

- 480cc reservoir built into the handle, helps to remove the moisture and prevent pulsing

- Pressure gauge

- Detachable air regulator for precise air pressure adjustment

- Working pressure from 1psi to 60psi.

- Comes with a 3 metre (10') vinyl hose

- Built-in spray-gun holder

- Size: 28 x 16 x 33cm

- Weight: 7.3kg

- Air flow: 1.4 CFM (40 lpm)

- Voltage: 220-240V

- One year warranty

The Silver Jet

The Iwata Silver Jet is the perfect companion to fine Iwata airbrushes such as cosmetics, tanning or body art. It's best suited to mobile or occasional use - about three to four applications per day.

The Silver Jet features:

- Low maintenance, oil-less single piston air compressor

- Quiet running 110W motor

- Comes with coiled hose and free Iwata Pistol Grip Moisture Filter

- Pressure gauge

- Pressure adjustment knob

- Built-in airbrush holder

- Cord wrap

- Working pressure from 10psi to 18psi.

- Size: 15.4 x 15.4 x 15.4cm

- Weight: 2.9kg

- Air flow: 0.33 CFM (9 l/min)

- Voltage: 220-240V 50Hz

- One year warranty.

Tents

A spray-tanning tent is needed for spray tanning, especially if you intend to take your services mobile. Regardless of how good your system is, and how skilful you yourself may be, can you really afford to take a chance on damaging a client's furnishings and possessions? Be aware that beach cubicles and changing tents are now being sold as tanning tents, so make your purchase from a reputable supplier.

Ideally your tent should have a clear roof, and the more windows the better; natural light will help in applying and assessing colour. When a tent is erected in a small room for instance, the inside of the tent becomes quite dark. If you're working without a bronzing agent you'll find things even harder.

You could buy a spray-tanning tent light, but bear in mind that if there isn't a plug socket within easy range you'll also need to take an extension lead.

The tent fabric should be stain-proof and waterproof, as a precaution against leakage onto floors. A quick wipe with a damp cloth at the end of a session will keep the tent itself clean.

Even in a salon tanning room, a spray tanning tent has its benefits; it localises the overspray, saving you time wiping down your room and cleaning your equipment. Cleaning becomes even easier when you use an extractor fan, as it'll keep the area and atmosphere almost entirely free of overspray. Overspray will always extract quicker in a tent, making breathing more comfortable for technician and client alike.

The extractor unit should be placed on the outside of the tent at the back, with the front-side filter of the extractor unit pushed right into the extractor gap/flap, as far as it will go, without it actually standing on the inside of your tent. The back of the extractor unit should be on the outside of the tent so it can blow the clean air back into your chosen working room. Never block the front or back of the extractor unit with the tent material or any other object as the extractor unit may overheat and even start a fire.

Some technicians do put the extractor unit in the tent, but that's a mistake. The clean air is then blowing into the tent and in turn blowing the overspray around, making it difficult for the extractor to do its job, making the air less comfortable to breathe and the tent rather chilly for the client to stand in.

It may seem an obvious point, but take a little care when erecting a pop-up tent. I've heard plenty of tales told about broken ceiling lights and china - and that sort of incident hurts your profits, your insurance premiums, your reputation, and it's just plain embarrassing and awkward.

Extractor units and fans

An extractor fan removes and filters overspray generated in the application of spray tanning solutions.

If you don't use an extractor unit, it's likely you and your client will be inhaling some of that fine mist, and it'll settle on walls and furniture. That's unhealthy and unclean. Fail to use one and you expose yourself to risk of cleaning bills, insurance claims and possibly worse if your client suffers asthma or has other breathing-related or eye-related problems. Even salon owners without any known respiratory problems have been known to suffer tightness of breath when spraying in rooms with poor ventilation.

There are a lot of extractor units on the market today, and having gone through five of them myself I've taken the time do some thorough homework.

You need a high-end extractor unit that clears as much overspray as possible.

Checklist

1. Firstly check how much overspray your extractor will clear per hour. The higher the m^3 (metres cubed), the more overspray it will clear. This does make a huge difference, although it may not seem significant. Some manufacturers give readings taken before the filter is fitted – that's misleading, since the m^3 drops quite a considerable amount when the filter is fitted. Since you'll need to compare like for like, ask if the extractor is tested filtered or unfiltered.

2. Check your extractor unit is CE-approved. By law, all extractor units should display the CE sticker, but some are still sold without it. Check your extractor unit is suitably certified/approved for the country in which it is to be used. CE-approved, for instance, will not necessarily be approved in the US. This is vital for electrical safety; if the equipment isn't right you risk electric shocks, damage to electrics and even fire.

3. European health and safety laws require the slots at the back of the extractor to be tested with a stainless steel finger the size of a small child's finger. Make sure that the slots won't allow small fingers to pass through the vents at the back of the extractor unit.

4. Extractor units can be awkward to carry around, due to their size and weight. Make sure you even consider their shape. If they are large, long and heavy, you'll bash your shins when you carry it. Oversized and heavy extractor units are the bane of a mobile technician's working day.

5. Make sure your extractor comes with a warranty. One year is normal, but you'd be surprised how many are being sold without one at all. A warranty should cover for a fault and not misuse. Paying the postage when returning a unit if a fault is found is quite normal, though it would normally be refunded if the fault is covered. The postage can work out rather expensive however if the manufacturer is in China.

6. Make sure the filter is washable. Replacing filters can get extremely expensive when you consider that some extractors' filters last only twenty tans. Check how thick they are. Some are paper-thin, so not only do they not last long but they'll also ruin the inside of your extractor, causing the motor to burn out with the volume of moisture being drawn in from the excess tanning solution. Washable filters should be washed every time you use your extractor, at the end of your day. Make sure you only put it back in the extractor when it's completely dry.

7. If you are buying a second-hand extractor unit, be careful you are not buying something that's worn out. As an essential item in spray tanning, extractor units are normally only replaced because their owners are upgrading to a better model or if they're falling to pieces.

8. Check the noise level of an extractor unit. Some rattle and are so noisy that your chat with your client becomes a shouting match.

9. Some extractor units claim to be made in England but are actually being bought as a kit from China and then assembled in England. They may not British made, but that's ok if they're CE-approved.

10. A closer examination of some extractor units may reveal large gaps on the inside of the extractor unit. The motor may claim to be a high m³ clearance, but those gaps mean that when put to work the unit can't clear the volume stated.

A high-end extractor unit: Microclene

This extractor unit is just a guide and I've used it as an example because of its quality. Weigh up its specification against any model you consider buying.

The specification:

- 75-watt motor, driving a backward curved fan for power and efficiency

- Over 750 cubic metres of air filtered an hour (equal to filtering a large double car garage 10 times per hour)

- Thermal protection with built-in cut-out

- Ingress protection to IP44 standards

- All steel construction weighing only 5.5kg

- Dimensions: 30H x 31W x 14D excluding handle and knobs

- Power coated for long life in black (oven baked)

- One year warranty

- CE-approved

- 230 volt, 75 watts

- Two-metre power cord

- Conforms to the small child's finger test as previously described

- Made in England to high standards.

The airbrush

I thoroughly recommend www.airbrushes.com for airbrushes and associated kits. It's a family-run business that's been about since 1947. I've met everyone at the company, and have found them to be uniquely helpful. What's more they're knowledgeable and can even undertake repairs.

Using your airbrush

Using the airbrush for applying tanning solutions is very simple, and the following applies to the separate dual-action airbrush gun and compressor system.

1. Firstly, the solution is poured from the large bottle into the suction feed colour pot. This in turn is secured to the airbrush.

2. Check your compressor pressure gauge is set between 10-12psi, measured while the airbrush gun is spraying. Psi = Pounds per square inch. 10-12psi is suitable for spray tanning with the single and dual action airbrush gun. 12-20psi is suitable for the LVLP gun. By keeping the pressure as low as possible on the compressor the droplets of solution will be wetter when applied to the skin.

3. Now push down the button on the airbrush and **gently** pull it back on its groove. As you do this, you will notice a fine spray coming through the nozzle at the front of the airbrush. Collect the sprayed solution onto a tissue.

Practise this exercise by spraying out onto a large sheet of kitchen towel or couch roll. Learn to control your airbrush gun and the amount of tanning solution that's being produced.

The aim is to produce a perfectly flat, **seamless** layer of spray tan. Hold the nozzle of the airbrush gun about 4-5 inches from the surface you're treating, and gently move the brush backwards and forwards horizontally, coating the area twice, then moving down a line, gently building up layers of colour with no stripes. The spray **must** be very even all over. Keep practising until you can do this perfectly.

It's a good idea to practise on family before you perform your spray tan on a paying client. Spend a couple of weeks getting your application onto skin flawless. Get your family's feedback on how the spray tan you applied performed.

- How long did the tan last?

- Did they get any patches?

- Did you miss anywhere?

- How were the feet, knees, elbows and hands when you applied their tan? These are very dry areas of the skin and you need to get the application right.

- Did they like the colour of their spray tan?

- Would they have this same spray tan again?

- Most of all, would they **pay** to have you spray tan them again?

Cleaning and maintaining your airbrush

Keeping your airbrush clean is the single most important aspect of owning an airbrush gun. The vast majority of airbrush problems are caused by a build-up of colour, which causes a blockage. Regular cleaning is absolutely essential. It should become second nature for you to always flush your airbrush gun with the appropriate cleaning agent after use.

Many technicians think they don't need to clean their airbrush every day that it is used, but actually you should clean your airbrush after every single tan.

If you don't clean your airbrush after every tan, it will start to underperform and you'll soon find yourself replacing the gun or even the entire system.

Simple day-to-day cleaning

All you have to do is:

- Begin cleaning by removing the airbrush feeder bottle and all tanning solution contained in the feeder bottle. Once the feeder bottle is removed, spray the solution that's collected in the feeder bottle spout into a tissue until the entire tanning solution has blown out.

- Put a little cleaning fluid into a clean feeder bottle and attach it to your airbrush gun.

- Spray a heavy volume of cleaning fluid through the gun.

- Place a tissue over the end of the airbrush gun so that the nozzle of the airbrush is blocked and this causes the fluid to bubble up in the feeder bottle as you flush.

- Remove the tissue from the end of the airbrush gun and flush through with more cleaning fluid until the cleaning fluid spray is running clear.

- Remove the feeder bottle from the airbrush gun and then spray again until no more cleaning fluid is present in the spout or blowing out of the airbrush gun.

- Now flush through with clean water, remove the water feeder bottle and again blow out the water that has collected in the feeder spout and airbrush.

- It takes around a minute to clean your airbrush correctly.

- Your airbrush gun is now ready to be put away or used again.

Major clean

Once a week it pays to give your airbrush a more thorough clean. Take it to pieces following the manufacturer's instructions. Clean your gun thoroughly with cleaning fluid and a lint-free cloth. For awkward places, including the nozzle, a small, stiff paintbrush can be used to remove the solution build-up. A small, longhaired hog stencil brush is ideal.

Cleaning fluid is a must for all airbrush gun equipment

There are many cleaning fluids on the market today that will keep your gun in tip-top condition, and depending on bottle size, they're very affordable. Get into the habit of cleaning your airbrush gun right from the start and your equipment will last far longer and perform much better. Keeping feeder bottles set up permanently in your work area, filled with cleaning solution and water, reminds you to clean your gun before and after every spray tan.

Alternatively, airbrush-cleaning foams are available. They should be squirted into your gun and left overnight to work into the thickened solution that will have formed in the gun. The next day you can add warm water to a feeder bottle, attach it to your airbrush gun, and flush through.

Golden rules for maintenance

- Do clean your airbrush regularly. Never allow the airbrush to stand long enough for the tanning solution to thicken and clog the gun. Repeated usage without cleaning will ruin your airbrush gun.

- Choose a work surface that is flat and well lit.

- Most important of all, if you are not sure what is wrong and don't know how to fix it, consult your airbrush dealer.

- The needles are very delicate and if bent, **will** need replacing. When taking the needle out of the airbrush to clean, **do not** push it back into the airbrush too hard; you'll damage the end needle tip and the airbrush nozzle will split. You should always keep a spare needle and nozzle, both of which are readily available from airbrush gun suppliers. Your needle must be specifically for airbrush tanning and is normally a 0.5 tanning needle, different from the nail art needle.

- Always have kitchen roll, tissue or couch roll at hand for cleaning spills, protecting flooring and blowing the spray tanning solution onto.

- You always start a spray tan by spraying onto the tissue first, and then, keeping your airbrush flowing, apply straight to the skin. This will help prevent any blots or freckles that your airbrush may blow out.

- At the beginning of a spray tan, a quick flush-through of the gun with your cleaning fluid, followed by a quick flush-through of water will help the gun stay in good working order. This procedure should help your spray tan application to be problem-free. This process also needs to be repeated on completion of the spray tan.

- Should the gun clog while performing a spray tan, flush it with water and not cleaning fluid. You should never use cleaning fluid while in the process of applying a spray tan in case any cleaning fluid is left in the gun spout or the feeder bottle. If that ends up on your client's skin he or she could suffer an adverse reaction.

An airbrush cleaning station is an extremely useful piece of equipment to own.

When flushing through your airbrush gun, you can prevent the spray from the cleaning fluids from being blown into your working atmosphere by directing the spray into this cleaning station. It's a controlled and more sustainable alternative to blowing fluids into tissue, and also serves as a handy airbrush holder.

Troubleshooting your equipment
Compressor

PROBLEM	DIAGNOSIS	SOLUTION
Compressor doesn't work or there is no air coming from the airbrush.	❑ Make sure it's switched on at the mains and on the machine itself.	Switch it on.
	❑ Check plug for faulty wiring and fuse.	Secure wiring and/or replace plug fuse.
	❑ Check for kinks in the hose, between the airbrush and compressor and inside the compressor case.	Un-kink hoses.
Compressor getting hot.	❑ Been running too long	Should cut out automatically if too hot, but if not switch off and leave to cool.
		Switch off when not in use.
		Consider changing your compressor to a larger model that can cope with the amount of tans you are doing.
Compressor gives little or no air pressure, or just keeps running.	❑ Are air hoses connected?	Ensure both ends of the air hose are tightly attached.
	❑ Are there any splits in the hose?	Replace hose.
	❑ Check pressure gauge.	Set pressure gauge to correct setting.
	❑ Check hose ends inside compressor case.	Tighten hose ends.

Troubleshooting your equipment
Dual action airbrush gun

Air coming out of airbrush gun, but blowing back into colour bottle and bubbling. No solution coming out of airbrush.	❏ Dirty airbrush.	Thoroughly clean airbrush.
	❏ Airbrush solution knob is wound all the way in.	Unwind solution knob to correct solution flow.
	❏ Needle nut not tight.	Tighten needle nut.
	❏ Needle and nozzle cap not tight.	Tighten needle cap and nozzle.
	❏ Pressure gauge low.	Turn up pressure gauge.
	❏ Airbrush needle is not seen in the nozzle and is not moving when trigger is pulled back.	Needle is stuck, so free needle and thoroughly clean.
No solution coming out of airbrush gun.	❏ Empty colour bottle.	Refill it.
	❏ Blocked nozzle.	Clean it.
	❏ Needle nut not tight.	Tighten it.
	❏ Blocked hole in bottle cap.	Use a pin to unblock the hole.
Airbrush application splatters.	❏ The needle may be hooked, damaged or dirty.	Clean or replace needle. Always keep a spare needle.
	❏ The nozzle may be dirty or damaged.	Clean thoroughly. See manufacturer's cleaning instructions. Change nozzle.
	❏ Poor needle position.	Make sure the tip of needle is coming out of the nozzle. Check needle nut is tightened.
	❏ Moisture filter is full.	Drain moisture filter.
	❏ Incorrect pressure.	Check pressure is correct.

Airbrush gun producing too much overspray.	❏ Room or tent foggy with overspray.	Turn solution knob on airbrush to reduce spray amount. Do not pull trigger too far back; adjust on gun so you cannot pull too far back. Your needle may be too far back; reposition as required. Make sure needle nut is tight. Needle may be dirty and stuck, requires cleaning. Check your compressor gauge is not set to high. Use an extractor unit to take overspray away.
Trigger does not move on the airbrush gun.	❏ You may have your solution control turned all the way in, so the trigger cannot be pulled back.	Turn it back up.
Trigger is floppy on the airbrush gun.	❏ Dirty/sticky needle	Loosen the needle nut and snap the trigger back into place. Clean needle and check it is clean regularly.
The feeder bottle is stuck in the airbrush gun.	❏ Solution has built up and caused feeder bottle to stick.	Grip the sides of feeder bottle connector with a spanner and undo. Squirt foam cleaner in where you connect the feeder bottle. Fill feeder bottle with water and flush your gun thoroughly. Turn your compressor up for a powerful flush-through.

Troubleshooting your equipment
Single action airbrush gun

Air is coming out of airbrush gun, but no tanning product is coming out. Or air is bubbling back into the feeder bottle.	❑ Make sure fluid adjustment knob is not wound all the way in. ❑ Make sure needle chucking nut is tight. ❑ Make sure needle cap and nozzle cap are tight. ❑ Airbrush dirty. ❑ Check pressure gauge is not too low.	Unwind. Tighten. Tighten. Thoroughly clean airbrush. Check gauge while spraying is around 10 psi
Too much spray is coming out of the airbrush.	❑ Your needle may be positioned too far back. ❑ Make sure needle chucking nut is tight. ❑ Check pressure gauge is not too high. ❑ Check fluid adjustment knob is not open too much.	Reposition it. Tighten it. Turn it down to around 10 psi. Close fluid adjustment knob to reduce spray.
The application is streaky and patchy	❑ Check for damage to needle or nozzle. ❑ Dirty airbrush. ❑ Check hoses are disconnected between sessions and when not in use. ❑ Check pressure gauge reads correct pressure while spraying.	Replace. Thoroughly clean airbrush. Disconnect when not in use. Turn pressure gauge up or down to read around 10 psi while spraying.
The bottle is stuck in the airbrush.	❑ Grip the flat sides of the bottle connector with a spanner, twist and pull free bottle.	Clean the bottle and airbrush thoroughly.
No air coming from airbrush.	❑ Check for kinks in the hose between airbrush and compressor. ❑ Check for kinks in the cooling hose.	Straighten hoses. Straighten hose.

If in doubt, or if you cannot put your problem right, contact your supplier or the manufacturer.

However, most of those problems can be avoided in the first place by cleaning and maintaining your equipment regularly.

The last thing you want is to have to go through this troubleshooting guide in the middle of a client's session. Follow the below maintenance schedule religiously.

- Keep all moving parts lubricated.

- Clean the airbrush every time you use it.

- Keep an eye on your moisture trap and drain when needed.

- Soaking the needle cap and nozzle in cleaning fluid for half an hour at the end of your working day will help minimise solution build-up.

- Turn the needle regularly so the needle wears equally.

- Keep all equipment switched off when not in use.

- Wipe your compressor over with a dampened cloth every time it is used, to stop solution overspray build-up.

- Foam cleaning fluids help to clean awkward places, and can be left in the gun overnight.

- A stiff-ish paintbrush can be used to clean hard to reach parts of the airbrush gun.

- Keep a spare spray tanning needle and nozzle handy.

It's a good idea to get your compressor and airbrush gun serviced every twelve months, but don't forget that you'll need a reliable back-up system while your equipment is away for servicing.

Diagram of Iwata Revolution SAR single action airbrush gun:

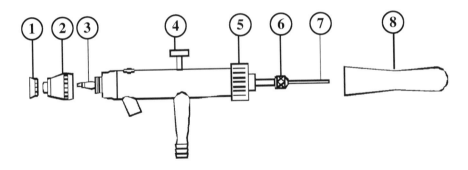

1. Needle cap: Protects the tip of the needle (7).

2. Nozzle cap: Protects the nozzle (3).

3. Nozzle: The tanning solution comes out through the nozzle.

4. Trigger: Press down for air and product.

5. Fluid adjustment knob: Adjusts the volume of product.

6. Needle chucking nut: Secures the needle (7) to the fluid adjustment knob (5).

7. Needle: As you turn the fluid adjustment knob (5) the tip of the needle (7) moves in or out of the nozzle (3) to allow more or less product through.

8. Handle: Remove for access to the needle (7) and needle chucking nut (6).

Diagram of Iwata Eclipse BCS dual action airbrush gun:

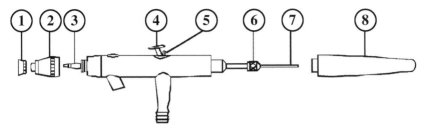

1. Needle cap: Protects the tip of the needle (7).

2. Nozzle cap: Air passes through the hole and draws liquid from the nozzle (3). Protects nozzle (3).

3. Nozzle: The tanning solution comes out through the nozzle.

4. Trigger: Press down for air, and then pull back for product.

5. Aux Lever: Moves backwards and forwards with trigger.

6. Needle chucking nut: Grips the needle (7) and moves with the trigger (4).

7. Needle: The tip of the needle moves in and out of nozzle (3) to allow product through.

8. Handle: Remove for access to needle (7) and needle chucking nut (6).

3

Spraying the body: preparing the client

Running a successful spray tan business in a salon or mobile doesn't just require the ability to spray a fantastic tan; it also takes exceptional customer care and service to keep your clients coming back to you.

Some clients may have reservations about having a spray tan applied and the best way to help your client relax is to explain to them what is involved with the application. Clients will quickly and easily relax when they know you are well educated and comprehensive in your knowledge of the spray tan application.

Supplying too much information on a website might lead to a client thinking your knowledge is not given as personal care. I don't believe in the saying 'time is money' because every client should have free adequate personal attention.

1. Exfoliation

Exfoliation is as important as the spray tan itself. Full exposure to the skin's protein surface is required for the spray tan to work. Without a good base the spray tan will not last. Clients should always be instructed to exfoliate and moisturise prior to receiving their spray tanning treatment. The most important areas to exfoliate are the elbows, knees, feet and ankles, hands and wrists and in between the toes and fingers. These areas tend to be very dry compared to the rest of the skin, and the spray tanning solution will often cling to these areas, causing noticeably darker patches when the spray tan has developed.

Exfoliation should be done two days prior to a spray tan, so the skin has adequate recovery time. Sensitive skin can be irritated by spray tan solution.

Exfoliation *can* be done the day before your spray tan, or continuous exfoliation treatments for a couple of days prior, if the skin is **not** very sensitive. This will give extra silky smooth skin - the exact base you need. For a good spray tan to develop, skin should always be moisturised after the exfoliating treatment with an oil-free moisturiser.

If your client does **not** exfoliate it could affect their spray tan, causing patching or fading to the developed result, so you need to make them aware of this before their spray tan application.

Cleansing and exfoliating the skin on a regular basis not only removes the dead skin cells, it also increases the blood flow and this in turn increases new cell activity and growth. If the skin is smooth and well moisturised, the tan will last a little longer. Subsequent moisturising after the spray tan has been applied is also beneficial. Dry, flaking skin is shed more quickly and so the tan will disappear prematurely. A good moisturiser will deliver water to the skin, keeping it hydrated, moist and supple, with the bonus of slowing down the natural aging process.

- Exfoliating is a must and this question should be on your consultation form.

- Moisturising needs to be done the night before a spray tan but if the skin has extra dry areas, moisturise **at least** 4 hours before so it doesn't act as a barrier to the spray tan solution.

- Moisturisers that contain oil and high alcohol content will prematurely remove the spray tan.

Alternatively, exfoliating treatments can be offered to the client at an extra cost and may include body brushing, scrubbing and polishing.

2. Hair removal

It is not necessary to shave or wax prior to spray tanning. Clients may however choose to do this, so if shaving is to be done with a razor, it should preferably be the day before so that the pores of the skin have time to close up. If the pores aren't closed, the spray tanning solution will settle and show up as freckled dots when the tan has developed.

Waxing should be carried out two days before the spray tan to give the skin adequate time to readjust itself. Waxing also acts as exfoliation and some spray tanning solutions may irritate the newly waxed skin.

All hair removal prior to spray tanning should be done after the exfoliating, as doing it the other way around may cause irritation to the skin. Again, moisturise afterwards.

If a client wants to shave with a razor after the tan has been applied, they should use a new, very sharp razor to reduce the number of strokes. Repeated motion over the same area can cause a spray tan to wear off prematurely or even cause stripes. Waxing after the spray tan has been applied will strip the tan.

3. Protecting the hair, eyes, nose and mouth

In principle it's not necessary to cover hair, since the tanning solution only reacts with skin, but solutions with high bronzing agents can turn bleached, fair and grey hair an orange colour. But hair should be tied up to ensure that the neck, back and shoulders are free of any strands which may interfere with the perfection of the spray tan. A headband can be used to keep the hair from the face.

If your spray tanning solution contains a high bronzing agent, cover your client's hair with a shower or spray-tanning cap or apply a barrier cream all round the hairline. Vaseline may be a little difficult to remove from the hair. A barrier cream should also be applied to the lips so that your client doesn't then lick his or her lips, and swallow any of the solution.

Eyes must be held firmly closed when spraying the face and small eye pads or winkies (disposable goggles) can be used if the client wishes to keep the lids free from colour.

Clients should hold their breath when the spray tanning solution is blown over the nose, or the tan spray will be breathed in. Nostril plugs would prevent this.

You, as the technician, should wear a mask and disposable latex gloves – no shortcuts!

4. Clothing

If possible, clients should be asked to wear loose fitting clothes, or at least bring some to put on after the tanning treatment. Tight clothing will rub the spray tan after the application and may slightly blemish the result. Residual colour from the bronzing agent may also be transferred onto the clothing if it's too tight, and although this can easily be removed in the wash, you can encounter problems with delicate fabrics such as nylon, satin and silk.

Clients should also bring their own towel if they have leather upholstery in their car or home. Leather is, as we've already established, skin, so the spray tan can discolour and stain these materials.

During the spray tanning treatment itself, clients will be asked to stand. For an all-over spray tan, a client's normal underwear is fine. Some clients may want to wear a bikini or accept the disposable underwear provided by the technician.

- It is important for the client to feel comfortable when they have their spray tan, so any choice of undergarments they want to wear should be acceptable. Ensure you tell the client of the pitfalls of wearing large pants and bras; but if they're happy with larger white areas from their underwear do remember that this is their choice.

- Recommend they wear old underwear to be on the safe side. Spray tan solution can be washed out, but a high bronzing agent may cause a discolouration to some materials; so good advice would be to wear black.

- If you supply disposable underwear, make sure it is your client that puts the underwear in the bin and not you, for the obvious hygiene reasons.

- Footwear can cause a spray tan to rub off prematurely, especially when it's newly applied, so the best tip is for clients to wear flip-flops.

- Bra straps can also rub away the tan, so prepare your client for this, and advise them not to wear straps on leaving.

4

Application: positioning the client

The process I'm about to describe is for precision airbrush tanning.

You should always explain to the client the procedure of a spray tan, never presuming prior knowledge, and always treating every client as a first-timer even if they've stated that they've had a spray tan before. You should also have given before-care advice for them to carry out with preparatory exfoliation before the tanning session.

Clients should always stand upright to receive the spray tan treatment, which should take no more than 20 minutes, including spraying and drying. Flooring may be protected with paper towels and a dark towel will protect the soles of the feet from collecting any spray tan solution which has settled on the floor from the overspray.

As we've already established, most technicians apply the spray tan within a spray-tanning tent; some use a shower cubicle or other tiled area where residual spray tan overspray can easily be cleaned away. Residual overspray is easily removed with a lightly dampened cloth and for the most part does not stain surfaces other than skin. Nonetheless, a tent and extractor unit will protect the immediate environment. Good ventilation is always required since residual spray tan overspray does escape into the atmosphere. It's harmless, but can become unpleasant if the air isn't given time to clear.

Before you start on any new area of the body, you must first check your gun's pressure and performance by blowing it onto a tissue.

Apply the spray tan approximately 4-5 inches away from the skin, depending on your airbrush gun. Get too close and you'll cause banding or stripes and if you're too far away you won't get good coverage, your solution will be wasted and there'll be plenty of overspray.

You should spray in sections; top half of the body first, and then the lower part, following the guidelines below.

1. Back

Starting from the top of the neck, gently waft the airbrush horizontally back and forth, working down towards the waist, then back up to the neck.

Apply a couple of extra coats of spray tanning solution around the underwear line, blending back up the body. You're looking to apply a good even coverage to the area you're spray tanning, this will give your client clear white underwear lines when the spray tan has developed. Take care not to get a wet look

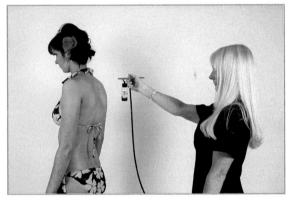

2. Right side

Ask the client to lift their right arm in the air. Now, starting from the armpit, gently waft the airbrush horizontally back and forth working down towards the waist and then back up again.

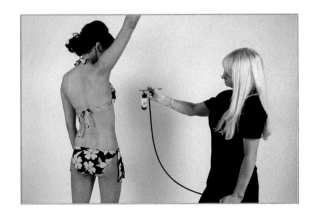

3. Front

Ask your client to place their arms horizontally out to the sides. Starting from the shoulders, follow the line of the collarbone before continuing down to the waist and back up again, making sure you continue with that horizontal wafting motion. Follow the natural shape of the bust with your airbrush as you glide over the chest area. Topless application will need the client's hands resting on their head; again you need to follow the natural curves of the bust with your airbrush, covering the entire chest area.

 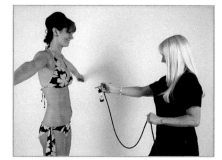

4. Left side

Ask the client to lift their left arm in the air. Now, starting from the armpit, gently waft the airbrush horizontally back and forth working down towards the waist and then back up again.

The four sections of the torso should now be completely airbrushed.

5. Arm application

Ask client to hold their arm out with their palm facing upwards. Start spraying on the diagonal, back and forth, working down the arm towards the wrist. **Do not spray the palm**. Then work back up on the opposite diagonal. This is known as cross-hatching.

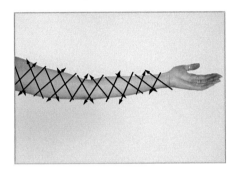
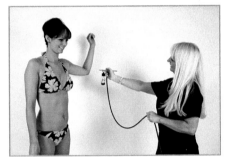

Next ask the client to turn the arm over so that the palm faces downwards and the fingers form a claw position. Now spray from the top of the arm, gently wafting back and forth on the diagonal, spraying lightly over the fingers. Work back up on the opposite diagonal.

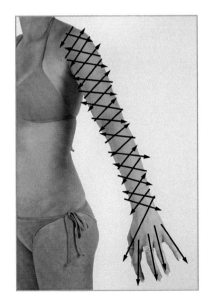
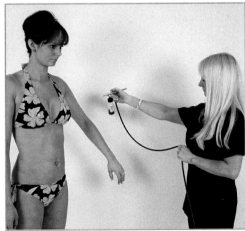

Instruct your client to bend their elbow, with the wrist turned so the hand is in a sideways claw. Now spray the outside of the arm, again using the cross-hatching method, down to the hand then back up again. Lightly spray over the elbow as this area tends to be quite dry and may otherwise absorb too much solution.

 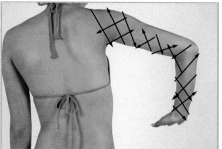

Finally, the client holds their hand and arm above their head while you gently waft up to the wrist, then back down using the cross-hatching method. It's important not to spray tan a heavy application over the hands, so if your gun's output can't be reduced you'll need to use a lighter faster action.

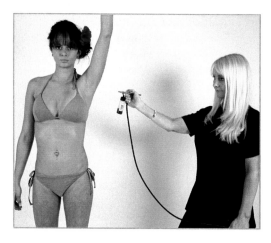 

6. Other arm

Repeat as stage 5.

7. Leg application

Imagine each leg is in four sections:

- Front inside of leg foot, turned right out to the side, which will then lead you onto spraying the:

- Middle front of the leg, foot facing forward, which will then lead you onto spraying the:

- Outside front of the leg (with the client turned to the side for you), which will lead you onto spraying the:

- Middle back to inside back of the leg, completing the application.

When airbrushing the legs, you should use the diagonal cross-hatching method used on the arms.

- Ask your client to stand with their right foot turning outwards. At this point you should be kneeling in front of your client.

- Starting from the knicker-line on the inside of the leg, waft diagonally down towards the foot and then back up again on the **opposite** diagonal. As with the hands, only a very light application of solution should be applied to the foot.

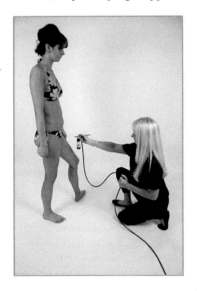 

- Next, ask your client to turn their foot towards you, and then start spraying again from the knicker-line down to the foot, then back up again using the crosshatch technique, and remembering to keep the application light when you reach the foot.

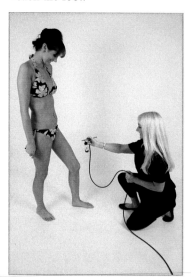 

- Get your client to turn around so you can treat the outside back of the leg. Starting at the knicker-line, continuing down to the bottom of the ankle, and once again cross-hatching.

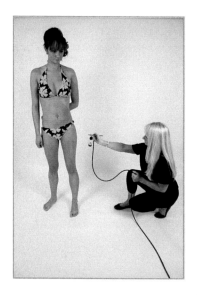 

- Finally, ask your client to put the left leg forward into the lunge position and spray the inside back leg in the same manner as above. You may need to add more sections as you go round, very common on the top of the leg, these extra sections, the application is exactly the same.

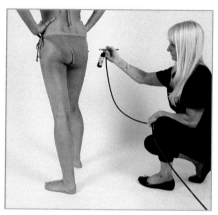

Care should be taken to make sure that the knicker-line area is treated well, so that when the tan has developed the client can see a clear white area from their underwear. If the application is too light around the knicker-line the client will not see a noticeable change of colour to their skin. It's possible your client may want a more blended effect however, so if you're unsure, feel free to check.

8. Other leg

Proceed as stage 7.

9. Face

Apply a barrier cream to the client's lips and provide nostril plugs and suitable eye protection. **These are sensible precautions to take**, as the effects of taking DHA internally are not known.

Wafting your airbrush back and forth horizontally, work down the face and neck, and then back up to the hairline. Don't forget to get your client to keep their mouth and eyes closed and hold their breath for a few seconds when you're spraying the lips and nose area.

10. Larger and mature clients

If you have never spray tanned a larger or mature person it can be a little difficult until you're used to their body. Concentrating on the application process used by your qualified tutor is going to be vital: listen to their advice and closely watch the speed of application, and the client's stances and positions.

Here are some straightforward tips to help you.

The solution sometimes collects in wrinkled skin and stays in a pool until it's dry, so lightly spray a few coats, letting the first coat dry before reapplying. If you **do** get a pool of spray tan solution, either dab it with a tissue or have a hair dryer set up to dry it off gently. You must make sure you spray tan in between any folds of skin if possible, so your client isn't left with white marks. A spray tan generally takes longer because you need to let places dry before reapplying the tanning solution and of course there are the extra positions required to stretch out the skin. Your normal routine will apply but you may need more working sections for each body part.

Larger clients often sweat more than the average person, so exfoliation becomes even more important. Be aware that if the client has perspired before the spray tan application takes place, the extra moisture contained in the skin may cause a barrier to the spray tan solution.

If your client has large breasts, spray tan the underside of the breasts first. For some, a simple stretch to the ceiling with both arms is enough, but others may need to lift their breasts for you. Spraying the stomach normally allows enough time for the underneath of the breasts to dry. Once the area underneath the breasts has dried, you can spray the top of the chest area. You should also warn the client that nearly everyone sweats under their breasts and the spray tan generally rubs off in this area quite quickly, especially when wearing bras.

When you've applied the spray to the cleavage and underneath the breasts and given the client a few minutes for the solution to dry, you may find that some solution is still sitting in the cleavage area of a larger client. You could give the client a piece of tissue folded into a long triangle. Place the top tip of the triangle in the centre of the cleavage and rest the longer ends of the tissue beneath the breasts, and then ask your client to lower her arms. This will just help to absorb any extra solution that may have collected.

Drying time

By the time you've finished the lower body, the upper body will be dry. Wait a further 5-7 minutes for the legs to dry. You can speed up the process with a hair dryer if required. The warmer the day or the room, the quicker the spray tan solution will dry.

The client can then dress and leave.

The entire process should take no longer than 20 minutes, plus 10-15 minutes in greeting, filling out a consultation form, undressing, dressing and paying. So aim to allocate around 30 minutes to each of your clients. If you are mobile, you'll also need to think about your travelling, set-up and pack-up times.

If your client wants a deeper tan, you can repeat the whole process as soon as the next day, but the first application should be washed off first with a light shower.

- Stage one lays the foundation and real tanning results will be apparent the next day.
  Stage one may not be enough unless the client is naturally darker skinned.

- Stage two develops the tan and makes it look two to three times darker.

- Arguably, you may never need to apply a stage two if you use decent tanning solutions and identify the correct tan tone percentage for each individual client. Knowing all about the product you use and how it performs will determine if a second application is likely to be needed.

You could always offer your client a tester tan with the product you use, to see if the tan they're hoping for is deep enough with just one application. You could either offer this on an introductory discount when switching to a new spray tan solution, or simply apply a small amount to a part of the body that's usually covered. Either way the next day you'll have your answer.

How to correct mistakes

The common mistakes you can make are:

1. Missing areas

2. Applying too much spray tanning solution

3. Applying uneven amounts of spray tanning solution.

Missing areas is down to carelessness. Concentrate on what you are doing and make sure you cover every inch, smoothly and evenly first time. Patches can be covered on the second application but may still be noticeable.

Applying too much spray tanning solution can happen quite easily. You'll know when this happens because the solution will begin to run. Either use a lint-free pad (kitchen towel or tissue) to lightly blot the oversprayed area or gently blow the area with a hairdryer and then re-spray the area lightly.

Applying an even spray tan is a matter of practice. Never apply too much tanning solution to any one spot. Do **not** try to paint the body brown. Gentle, methodical (loose wrist action, with a repeated routine) spraying is the key.

You need to find your own perfect application method and gently swaying does help a little until you feel comfortable with your airbrush application action.

Do not rush the process, but neither should you take too long; this spray tanning technique should take 15-20 minutes. Not concentrating on what you are doing because you are having a conversation may cause some, or all of the above. Practise, practise, practise.

Partial tans

Clients often ask for selective spray tanning to legs, arms, chest, back, shoulders, neck or face. Disrobing may not always be necessary and in such cases remember to cover your client's clothing with paper towels to prevent overspray settling on garments. Exfoliation, moisturising and so on are still fundamental requirements even for partial tanning, and the two-stage treatment may be necessary to develop a deeper spray tan if you're starting on pale skin, depending on the solution used and tan tone percentage.

I'm not a fan of partial tans, for several reasons: it takes almost as long to do as a full body tan; there's the risk of damage to a client's clothing; many clients who ask for the partial tan end up wishing they'd had the full tan once they've seen the results;

and finally it's tricky to come up with a cost with which everybody's happy. So if possible I'd recommend encouraging your client to be brave and go for the full tan.

Top-up tans

A spray tan starts to fade as soon as it is applied, but that's true of any tan, natural or artificial. Spray tanning, however, looks really good for up to ten days depending on the client's skin type the quality of your spray tanning solution and how well the before and aftercare advice has been observed.

Top-up tans can be applied up to six days after the first application to bring back the full colour achieved.

Overspray

There will always be overspray when using tanning solution. To minimise this, make sure you never work with more pressure from the compressor than is necessary; never work further away from the body than you need to (4-5 inches); and keep your airbrush in good clean condition. Following these simple rules should bypass most of the causes of overspray.

Make sure the area you choose for spraying is warm and well ventilated. Warmth helps the solution to dry quickly, and ventilation will clear the air of overspray and fumes.

In a busy salon or mobile tanning party, where one application follows another in rapid succession, fumes can build up and good ventilation and air circulation becomes extremely important. There are reports of adverse reactions to excessive spray tan solution inhalation, even among salon owners. There are even dishonest people out there who might make false allegations. So make sure your consultation form asks the question "Was an extractor unit was used on your visit today?" That way at least you can prove you did everything in your power to keep the client free from any risks of being unwell.

Make sure the area you select for working is free of soft furnishings. The best location would be a bathroom or similar enclosed washing area, where the walls are smooth and easily cleaned. Overspray will still settle on surfaces, but can be easily removed with a lightly dampened cloth. Carpets, flooring and other absorbent surfaces should be protected with paper towelling or paper sheeting.

Using a tent will contain most of any overspray produced and adding an extractor unit will not only minimise overspray further but make for a more comfortable atmosphere for you and your client.

Stand your client on a towel to avoid the overspray getting on the feet and when you've finished your spray tan, squirt the floor with antibacterial cleaning fluid and wipe it with a dark coloured towel. Alternatively you can use Sticky Feet to help stop the overspray collecting on the soles of the feet.

HVLP applications

HVLP application stances are almost the same as those taken during airbrush application, but the whole procedure is very fast – usually between 5 and 8 minutes for a full spray tan. The majority of HVLP guns should be held 6-8 inches away from the skin during spraying, but find out from your equipment supplier what their recommended application distance should be. HVLP machines vary in motor power, spray patterns, noise and also in the amount of solution used per application. It may be an idea to compare these before you buy.

HVLP spray tanning is very well suited to salon use as the application is fast, so the equipment can cope with continuous clients walking through the door. As discussed in the HVLP equipment section on page 27, HVLP application can produce more overspray and so cut into your profits since you'll probably use more solution per application. If you're using HVLP as a mobile technician you'll need to take extra care in your clients' homes; more overspray could lead to cleaning bills if you're not well prepared. Spray tanning tents and extractors are vital when you're taking your services mobile.

There's no right or wrong way to start the HVLP spray tan application. You can start with the client facing you, but starting on the back of the body can help your client to relax and get used to the situation, especially with topless applications.

If you position the client facing you, begin the application as follows:

1. The Torso

The tan should be applied in an upward-downward, fast motion, similar to the way you might paint a wall. Make sure your HVLP equipment is spraying in a light, even flow, as this will reduce the risk of streaking and smearing.

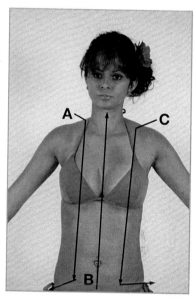

A. You should start and stop the spray tan application away from the body. The vertical movements start above the shoulder and proceed down in a straight line to the underwear line. Your gun should be approximately 8 inches away from the skin unless your equipment supplier's recommendations are different.

You can carry on straight down the front of the leg if you wish, in one continuous movement to the ankle, leaving the foot free from application, but these diagrams show stopping at the underwear line. Make sure that when stopping your gun stops away from your client's skin.

B. You continue moving your HVLP gun, so no overlapping is produced, and spray from the underwear line back up to the collarbone, underneath the chin and then away from the skin.

C. Repeated as A.

If your client is a larger person, you may need to repeat these movements until the torso is completely sprayed.

If your client is topless then they should raise their arms and rest their hands on their head. This helps to spray tan under the breasts, so that no visible area is left unsprayed and no white lines left behind .As with the airbrush application, if your client has large breasts, they should hold their arms above their head, pointing them straight to the ceiling; this gives a little more lift to the chest area.

Your movement should follow the natural shape of the bust, holding the HVLP gun vertically. The breasts are curved, so your HVLP gun will need to follow this shape. You only need to angle your hand slightly to follow the curves of the body, if you tilt the HVLP gun, you may cause a spillage from the breathing hole in the feeder bottle.

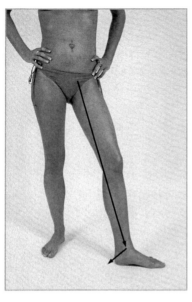

Legs should be sprayed next. The stances for leg application are the same as airbrush application, but HVLP is again applied in long vertical motions.

2. Starting from the underwear line at the top of the inner leg, spray tan straight down to the ankle. Don't spray tan the feet at this stage. You need to pull your gun away from the skin as you approach the ankle.

The overspray produced from the HVLP while spraying the legs, can settle on the feet. For this reason, and because the feet have a tendency towards dryness, you should never apply the same kind of quantity to feet.

3. When you have sprayed the inside-front of the leg down, you'll need to repeat the process in exactly the same way on the inside of the opposite leg.

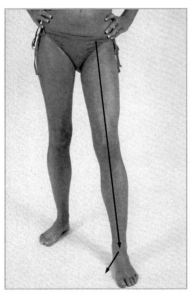

4. The front of the leg application is applied with the client's leg facing straight towards you. From the underwear line, glide your gun straight down to the ankle, again missing the foot by moving the gun away from the leg at ankle height, while still spraying.

Bending the knees slightly, as with the airbrush application, helps to stretch out the creases around the knee. The tanning solution needs to cover these creases or you'll end up producing white lines. Again it's best to pull the HVLP gun away a little from the skin on the knee – because the skin is often dry here you can end up producing too dark a tan.

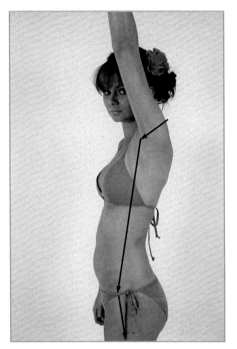 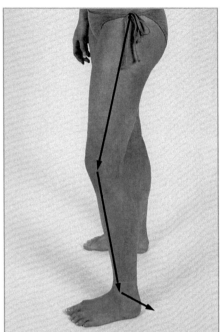

5. The side of the body is sprayed at the same time as the outer side of the leg, so the client should raise their arm above their head, so you can glide the HVLP gun from the back of the armpit down over the underwear, and straight down to the ankle, again pulling away from the skin at the ankle. Make sure that all your tanning applications meet seamlessly, with no banding or overlapping.

Do not let your client lower the raised arm until the spray tan is dried - they can rest their hand on their head for comfort.

6. Spray tan the opposite side of the client, in exactly the same manner as in step 5.

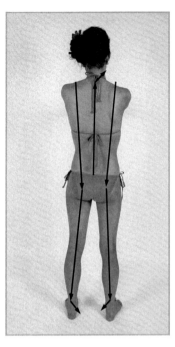

7. The back of the torso should be spray tanned at the same time as the back of the legs, again making sure all your applications join up. If your client isn't a jealousy-inducing size 6 you may need additional applications as we've discussed before.

Starting from the top of the shoulder, glide down the right-hand side of the back, over the underwear and straight down the back of the leg to the ankle. Stop the spraying off the skin as previously described.

Your client should hold their arms out in front; this gives a slightly rounded back and can prevent shoulder blade banding or stripes. If your client is wearing a thong then glide over the buttocks, slightly tilting your hand to follow the curved shape of the bottom. To spray tan the smile lines beneath the buttocks, get your client to lean or lunge slightly forward on each leg.

8. The centre of the back is spray tanned by gliding the HVLP gun straight up from the underwear line, as far as the hairline on the neck, at which point you'll need to move the still-spraying gun away from the skin.

9. The left-hand side of the back will include the left-hand side of the back of the leg, repeated as in step 7.

10. The inside back of the leg: glide from the underwear line straight down to the ankle, missing the feet, then repeat on the inner side of the opposite leg, in the same stance.

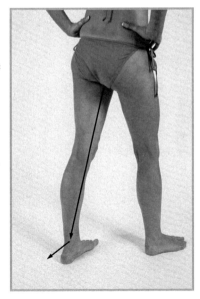

The arms are spray tanned in 3-4 sections, depending on the size of the arm and the spray pattern your gun produces to cover the area in any single spray.

11. Inside of the arm: you'll be tanning from the armpit to the wrist. Lightly coat the armpit and pull your gun away as you approach the wrist.

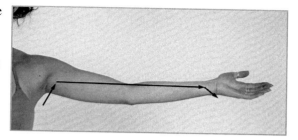

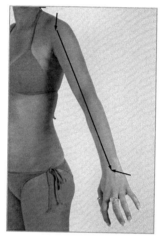

12. Top of the arm: start away from the body as usual and glide along the top of the shoulder straight down to the hand, pulling away as you reach the hand.

13. Back of the arm: with the client's elbow slightly bent, start away from the body and then glide from the top of the shoulder over the back of the arm, making sure the application is light over the elbow.

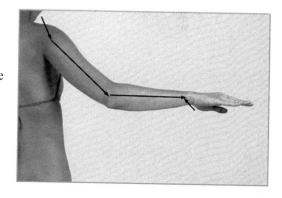

14. Underside of the arm: the client needs to hold their arm straight up above the head, while you spray from wrist down to armpit. This application may not be needed unless the client has larger arms. Be careful of over application to neck, should you need to spray this extra section and make sure the clients face is turned away from the overspray.

15. Face: Your client must close their eyes while you're misting the face. Once again the application is applied in fast vertical movements; don't forget to spray the neck area and both sides of the face. Depending on how much solution your HVLP equipment produces, the gun can be held further away from the skin than during the body application. Barrier cream should be applied to the lips, a mop cap worn to protect the hair, and it's recommended that clients wear a nose plug.

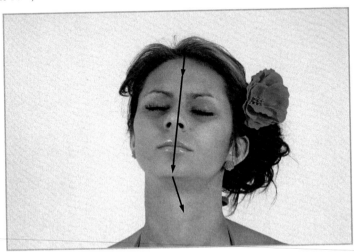

Repeat on both sides of the face.

Please don't forget to tell your client when they can breathe again if you are not using nose plugs.

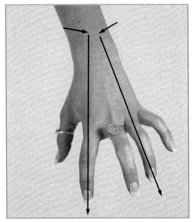

16. Hands: the hands can be lightly sprayed, but with HVLP it's not always necessary to spray them at all, as the overspray tends to fall over the hands from the arm application. If your routine includes spraying the hands, the client needs to make the shape of an upside-down open claw, as this will allow the tan to be applied in between the fingers. If you cannot turn down the amount of product your HVLP system releases, apply from further away than you would for the body application. Barrier cream should be applied to the finger nails to avoid staining.

17. Feet: a very light misting can be applied over the feet if needed, but again it's often not necessary with the HVLP application due to overspray from the leg application. Should the feet need spraying, make sure you apply the spray tan very lightly over this sometimes very dry area. You may need to spray tan the sides of the foot, depending on your gun pattern and how much area it will cover.

The whole body can be repeated, following the same routine, to make sure you haven't missed any areas. This may not be needed if your first application used the ideal spray tanning solution for your client's skin type, your application was even and light and the client's body doesn't have a wet appearance. This may depend on your HVLP system - some systems can act as a dryer.

General practice advice

- Keeping a checklist by the phone detailing every question you need to ask a client is extremely handy. You can then send any necessary information by post or email in advance of the appointment.

- If you don't want the expense of Sticky Feet, stand your client on a dark towel. In an emergency good kitchen roll or couch roll can be used.

- Make up samples of other products you sell that complement your services: spray tan extenders, exfoliants, moisurisers etc. Clients don't necessarily want to pay out for full bottles they've not tested, so sample pots allow them to find out what suits them best. Just divide your larger bottles up and create free samples. Being thoughtful can pay dividends further down the line.

- Always buy your tanning solutions from a reputable supplier. You may pay a little more, but at least you can count on the quality of the product. Not all tanning solutions bought online, for instance, are what they claim to be. Some are diluted, and others have been stored incorrectly and don't meet their shelf life. When you are buying online, pay close attention to any feedback sections on the websites you're browsing.

- Make sure you keep a spare airbrush system, even if it's one you buy second-hand. Never risk a situation in which you're partway through spraying a client and your system packs up. Not just embarrassing at the time; this scenario will be relayed to your client's friends, and that's bad publicity that could cost you dearly.

- Never try out new or unfamiliar products on a client first. Always check you're happy with the results by applying to your own skin, or close family or friends several times.

- A uniform always looks professional and saves ruining and wearing out your other clothes. Brand your uniform with your company name and you'll be advertising every time you pop to the shops. A simple name badge will do, but an embroidered logo looks very professional.

- Be friendly, but without compromising your professionalism. You need to make your clients feel relaxed, not self-conscious. Silence at the point of near-nudity can be extremely uncomfortable, so describe the work you're about to do, make polite small talk and consider playing music quietly in the background. Mobile technicians could even use a mobile phone to provide quiet musical accompaniment, just to save on lugging yet more equipment around.

❑ If your tanning solutions are nearing the end of their shelf life expectancy, consider running a promotion, such as two spray tans for the price of one, or bring a friend and divide the cost between them. If one client is going to take option 1, bear in mind the length of time between tans. Great publicity and no wasted product.

5

Bride and prom precautions

Almost everyone likes to look tanned and spray tanning is especially popular for special occasions. One session of spray tanning is said to be equivalent, colour-wise, to about six to eight sunbed sessions. For those who don't tan well naturally or who prefer to avoid the risks of skin cancer, a spray tan is particularly appealing.

Things to watch out for…don't ruin a special day

Most spray tan solutions have a bronzer present and although it's great that the client can walk away with an instant tan, for a bride or prom princess it could be a disaster.

There's a chance of streaks, patches and banding if the client did not prepare fully before the spray tan, or bronzer could settle into skin pores and create a freckled look. So it's your responsibility to make your client aware of all possible outcomes if they don't follow your advice.

It doesn't matter if the client does everything right if the application of the spray tan isn't good enough; so if you don't have adequate experience, please don't ruin a bride or prom princess's day. Sometimes turning them away until you have mastered your technique is better than earning yourself a bad reputation and being the talk of the wedding day or, worse still, the talk of your town.

When the bride or prom princess sweats in her dress she could produce brown stains on the inside of her outfit, especially in the places that her dress is tight. Most stains will come out, but it's difficult to remove stains from silk or satin. If the dress is hired there may well be cleaning costs, so you need to advise clients accordingly.

Your client could have her wedding or prom spray tan with a clear solution (no bronzer present), but only offer this option if you are an experienced spray tanning technician, so you can be sure you won't give a patchy tan.

If you and your client both decide to use the tanning solution with a bronzer present, then one way to help protect the dress on the special day is to lightly dust the body with talcum powder, using a powder puff. When the bride or prom princess sweats, commonly around the chest and waist, the talcum powder will absorb some of the moisture and the colour. **This will only help and not prevent colour leaking**. The bride or prom princess could keep their powder puff in their bag for top-ups during the day for these areas.

A dark tan doesn't always look convincing with a white or ivory wedding dress if the client is naturally fair skinned. Explain this to your client and try to persuade her to take a trial tan if she's set on a darker shade.

A trial spray tan for a wedding or prom should be done at least a month before the special day so that the tan has time to wear off and you have time to try another tan tone percentage if the first attempt wasn't perfect. The effect you should be aiming for is a golden, subtle tan, so that guests comment on how radiant she looks and not whether she's wearing fake tan.

Spray tan solution is a cosmetic and it's best to know beforehand how it will react with your client's skin. Allergic reactions are quite rare but nevertheless you should take no chances and insist on a patch test if the client has never had a spray tan before.

Prom princesses and young bridesmaids may find it a little difficult financially to have a trial spray tan if they are funding it themselves; so you could consider offering special rates for prom season or multiple bookings. Make sure that any under 18s have a parent present, a parental signature on the consultation form and the client should stay in full underwear unless the parent says otherwise.

A spray tan generally takes about 24 hours to develop fully, so if your client is having their wedding in the morning, it's best to give the spray tan time to set properly over the previous day. An early morning application would be wise, unless your client is used to spray tans and how to look after them correctly. Two days before their special day would give extra time for any repairs; especially sensible when dealing with a client without experience with maintaining a spray tan.

You could advise your client to make the most of the trial spray tan by trying their dress on (after a shower, obviously) to get family or friends' opinion on the colouring. It's even worth having a picture taken since photographs can come out a different colour.

It's vital that you record the tanning solution and tan tone percentage used for each client, so everyone knows which solution to use or **not** use on their return visit. There's no point in a trial if you can't remember what to use for the big occasion itself.

Booths are a quick and easy spray tan fix, but many are self-operated and no professional advice is given on colour tones and solution types. The application can be poor depending on the model of booth and if the client doesn't assume the necessary stances correctly then an uneven tan is possible. If the booth hasn't been maintained to the highest standards of hygiene, then there's the risk of coming away with Legionella bacteria that can grow in the automatic wash-cycle holding tanks. It's my view that bridal and prom spray tans should be applied using the separate airbrush gun and compressor method for an important day.

The effect of a nice, light to medium spray tan will make the eyes sparkle, the hair shine, make teeth appear whiter and complement the detail of the dress.

Brides and prom princesses often have their hands and feet on show for photos so you really need to keep their application light over these sometimes very dry areas and the importance of before care impressed upon your client. After the spray tan has been applied you can gently dab your client's hands, feet, cuticles, fingers, toes and knuckles, but if you've kept the application lighter over these areas it shouldn't be necessary. Concentrate on wiping their palms and under their feet if they have touched themselves or not been standing on a towel or sticky feet. It might be worth applying a barrier cream beforehand to help protect some of these areas.

If you've followed all this advice closely, you'll be adding an important finishing touch to somebody's very special day.

6
Spray tanning men

Most men look good with a tan and spray tanning for men is definitely on the increase. The greatest effect you get with many male clients is that the way colour accentuates muscles, especially the abdominals. That's exactly why body builders make tanning a key part of preparation for a competition.

Men usually have more body hair than women.

This won't come as a surprise, but if you've never spray tanned a man before, you may be surprised by the difference it makes to the process. For more hirsute gentlemen, turn your airbrush down and spray a lighter coverage over the body, still following your established routine, and repeat the application at least twice. If you hold the airbrush at a slight angle, it blows the hairs to the side, allowing the solution to get under the hairs better. Make sure you let the solution dry before repeating, as the hairs may still affect how much solution goes straight onto the skin. Lightly spray the whole body and by the time you return to your starting point the skin will be dry enough to repeat the whole application. It's a good idea to practise on a partner or male friend to get it right.

Having a hairy body doesn't usually affect the tan, but if the client is particularly hairy in areas such as the chest and legs, you'll get tiny beads of spray tan solution collecting. Once the application is complete you can dry off any excess with a hair dryer on a low setting. Gently dabbing with kitchen towel or tissue should be avoided on a male client.

Men's skin needs more spray tanning solution

Unless the male is very fair skinned, you can use a darker tan tone percentage than you might have chosen for a female client. Men tend not to use so much, or indeed any sun cream when sunbathing, so they often start with a good base in their natural skin colour. Darker spray tans don't seem to age men as much as they do women. What's more, in most instances male skin seems to absorb less tanning solution than a woman's, but while all this suggests that a darker solution should be ok, be sure to discuss and choose the tan tone percentage together with your client.

Saying all that, if a male client wants a spray tan for his wedding, suggest a trial run just as you would a bride; again the lighter spray tan does seem to look best in the photos.

You can charge a little more for a male spray tan as they usually need more solution and application generally takes a little longer. Do explain why the price is higher when you take their booking.

What if a male client has dark arms and face while the rest of his body is snow white?

If a male client has the famous English vest look - naturally tanned to the arms and face but with white body and legs - selective partial tans can be offered. Choosing the appropriate tanning system will depend on the amount of white area to be sprayed

Most HVLP systems tend to produce a wide, heavy and fast application of the solution. This type of application may overlap the already tanned natural skin, causing the same effect the male client already had, once the tan has developed.

You can achieve this type of partial tan easily with the handheld precision airbrush tanning technique, with no overlapping on the natural skin. A skilled technician will be able to match the white areas to the naturally tanned part of the body. Your knowledge of your solutions will tell you which tan tone percentage to use.

Your male client can of course have a spray tan in a tanning booth, but there'll still be a noticeable difference, even if he goes for a double-dip.

If your male client is balding

Please don't forget to spray tan your male client's balding head; few things would look sillier or more obviously fake than a lovely brown body and a white bald spot or head. If your client opts for a booth, he'll need to forgo the shower cap.

Do remember that some spray tanning solutions contain high amounts of bronzer and this could colour bleached, fair or grey hair to point-and-stare orange colour. For that reason it might be best to use a clear solution (no bronzer) for a male's balding head, but remember that if you use the tanning solution without a bronzer on the head, and the body application has been applied with bronzing agent present, then the client will leave you with a bronzed body, and white head until the tan develops about five hours later.

Most men feel more comfortable in a booth

Reports suggest that 80% of males would choose a spray-tanning booth over lay-down sun beds now.

The reason, it seems, is that a tanning booth is fast, easy and quite discreet, with no need to strip for a technician. A spray tan booth takes little more than a couple of minutes, whereas the gun method takes around 20 minutes.

But while that may be the preference, spray tanning for men is definitely a growth area, so if you're comfortable working with male clients, there are profits to be made.

Some crucial advice when applying a male spray tan

If you want to spray tan men, whether in your salon or in their homes, **please** make sure you have someone with you; if the client's own partner isn't there, then a girlfriend of yours. Your client should understand that this is for safety reasons, and if he objects then I strongly advise that you don't book or perform the treatment.

Back in 2001 there was no disposable underwear available, and the only way you could avoid white bottoms was by providing a towel for the client to hold over their private areas.

I had one extremely bad experience with a man who got terribly excited by the feel of the airbrush... And I'm not joking... I didn't know what to do apart from stop the spray tan every time this towel started to rise and wait for him to lose his excitement. Then it popped up again and I would stop and start again, and this carried on for what frankly seemed like forever. It was like a magic act you'd see on the TV, only it wasn't anything as appealing as a dove or a baby rabbit appearing from the towel.

I felt I couldn't stop the spray tan and leave because all my equipment was set out and he was half airbrushed. For all I knew might have sued me... I'd only been spray tanning mobile for a few weeks and back then there were no advice books, websites, phone lines, or even other girls to talk to. I was one of the first to qualify and I really did learn everything, well, the hard way.

I tried to act as professionally as possible, but I was really uncomfortable with the situation. No one had warned me that this might happen, and perhaps nobody had yet experienced this scenario. So this is my warning that it **can** happen, so you've been warned!

When I look back on this episode, although it now seems really funny, I realise that this situation could easily have turned into a far worse experience. I might have been propositioned; the client could have forced himself upon me; and there could even have been other men in the house too. With hindsight I can see I was terribly naive and even though I was already a black belt in full-contact kickboxing, I'd put myself in a potentially extremely dangerous position.

When you're tanning mobile, whether for male or female clients, always tell someone where you are going and at what time, and keep your mobile phone switched on at all times. If you can, have a phone number you can access by touching a single number on your mobile. Don't have your phone locked so you have to fumble around if you get into trouble, and keep your phone in your pocket at all times, **not** in your bag.

If you are going to a new area you can always use Google Maps to familiarise yourself. When you've typed in the address on Google Maps, you'll see a little gold man at the top of the zoom in and out function. If you click and drag the little gold man over to your searched address on the map, and drop him on the chosen street, you'll see the road, house and surrounding area by photo. This gives a good impression of the kind of area you'd be visiting, so you can always cancel an appointment if you feel it doesn't look safe.

If you have a salon, I'd recommend going to the trouble of having panic buttons installed: one near your till and another in your tanning room. These are surprisingly cheap to install and could help alert someone if you ever get into trouble. The noise should be enough to stop any trouble dead, but I'd recommend adding in the loudest scream you can possibly produce and some flying arms and legs too.

Women who run their salons where they're mostly alone are an easy target for burglars and strong personality males. You'd be surprised how word gets around. **Protect your day's takings and yourself**.

Spray tanning men is on the increase but just prepare yourself for what could happen, I have the towel to prove it!

7

Applying self-tanning products by hand

Applying self-tanning products by hand

Tan enhancers (self-tanners) are very popular post-tan and an excellent product to market. Teenagers in particular love self-tanning and they're spoilt for choice at a cost that most can afford. Self-tanners may not quite match the effect achieved by a well-applied spray tan, but they're great for keeping a natural tan topped up through the summer and easy to get used to.

Mastering self-tan application by hand comes with practice, patience and preparation. Your skin preparation should follow the same steps as for spray tanning, and so should your actions immediately post-tan:

- Any shaving should take place the night before to prevent tanning lotion pooling in your hair follicles

- Shower and exfoliate carefully to rid your body of any oils and dead skin

- Use a pH-neutral soap to bypass the streaking effect possible when oil is present

- Don't moisturise after your shower; with the possible exception of applying a very small amount to extremely dry areas such as elbows and knees

- Make sure you're fully dry after the shower. Using a tan enhancer too soon after moisturising or showering will prevent the DHA from bonding

- Don't sit on furniture or light clothing while the tanning solution is still damp on your skin

- Wear lightweight gloves to avoid telltale brown stains along fingernails, between the fingers and on your palms.

- For full details on skin preparation head back to chapter 3: Spraying the body: preparing the client.

Follow these rules rigidly and you should avoid all streaking, dotting and patching, or the embarrassing orange palms, knees, elbows and feet.

Just as with spray tanning solution, all self-tanners contain a chemical called Dihydroxyacetone (DHA), which temporarily stains the epidermis of the skin. If you don't apply the tan enhancers right to begin with, it's hard to stop the browning process once it starts; normally within an hour or so.

With that in mind, choosing the wrong shade for your natural skin tone will result your fake tan looking too orange to be believable. Just as with spray tanning, no two people will get the same tan from any one product.

So find the perfect shade for you, perhaps by testing it on an area of your body which is usually covered up. If your natural skin tone is very dark you should be able to use a dark tan enhancer, but it may be wise to start with fair or medium, and then change if the colour isn't strong enough for you. Naturally fair-skinned people should always start off with a product that has a lower concentration of DHA, ie a lighter tone, and give themselves two or three applications, spread out over a few days. Choose a tan enhancer that allows you to gradually build up your colour, no matter what your natural skin tone, over a number of applications.

Be careful about using a product that's been sitting in the cupboard longer than you remember. Many tan enhancers have a shelf-life of about two years, which includes the time the product sat in the store.

When applying the tan enhancers, work fairly quickly, making sure you rub the product in completely. Use the palms of your hands rather than your fingers, which can create a subtle but visible striping effect.

It's best to work from the feet upwards, since you'll need to bend down, and doing that with a freshly tanned tummy risks the product pooling into your body's creases. Having a routine is an excellent idea as you'll remember exactly where you've covered.

The most sensible routine is as follows:

1. Upper part of the feet, avoiding the sides and soles

2. One leg, front and back

3. The second leg, front and back

4. Buttocks and then belly

5. Your back and sides (ideally you should have someone else apply the tanning

product to your back, but if that's not an option, try attaching a sponge to a loofah - elastic bands work fine – and apply a well-judged quantity of the product to the sponge)

6. Chest

7. One arm

8. The second arm

9. Neck and face (blending the solution subtly into the hairline and lightly behind the ears and neck so as to avoid those telltale white marks

10. The backs of your hands and fingers. Always leave these until last, use a fairly light quantity of product and avoid staining between your fingers and palms. If you've been wearing gloves, remove one glove and apply to the back of this hand, then replace the glove and repeat the process for the opposite hand.

Tanning mits or gloves are of course ideal, but if you've not got any available, make sure you apply a barrier cream to your hands and let it soak in for 5 minutes before you start. Regular use of the barrier cream, following a quick hand-wash and another five-minute drying period, throughout your self-application will stop colour build-up on the palms of your hands.

If you're prone to streaks, try using a self-tanning cream or lotion, as opposed to quick-drying mousses or sprays, as they'll give you more time to smooth out uneven areas before they start drying. Self-tan enhancers with built-in tints also work to minimise the risk of streaking as you can see exactly where you've applied the lotion.

You can make your tan more intense by applying another coat of tan enhancer an hour after your first application, but do remember that if the product chosen is too dark for your natural skin tone, it will fade in an uneven fashion and look patchy and unnatural. For the first time, I'd recommend sticking to just the one application so you can be sure of how your skin will react.

If your tan has developed in streaks and is too dark, you can lighten the tone by wiping the entire area with a flannel soaked in lemon juice and a little salt. Specialist tan removers are also available from specialist suppliers, if you've really gone too dark. However, don't get carried away: please do a 24-hour patch test on your skin to see if you react to the tan removers. Just slapping these removers straight onto skin made sensitive by recent exfoliating and shaving could lead to unsightly rashes. Do remember though that neither tan removers nor lemon juice are guaranteed to remove the entire tan; it's likely they'll just lighten it.

A few other handy tips:

Tips:

- Excess solution can be removed using a paper towel or damp cloth.

- Rubbing a little moisturiser into wrists and ankles can assist with blending.

- Fingernail polish remover can be used to remove any nail staining that may have occurred.

- Nail polish, on the other hand, can be applied to fingers and toes to prevent strange brown marks appearing in the first place.

- Allow at least ten minutes post-tan to dry before throwing on clothing, and make it dark and loose-fitting when you do so. Wear loose pyjamas to bed to avoid staining the sheets. Do check your specific product for drying times as some can be longer.

- Unless you're using a rapid-tan formula that explicitly states quicker development times, wait at least 8 hours before showering. If you're especially fair-skinned and this is your first application, you may want to shower after 4-6 hours to ensure the tan doesn't develop too dark for your liking and skin tone.

Follow the same post-tan body care principles I described in chapter 12: Aftercare, and look out for the tan-damaging products described in the *Patchy and faded spray tans* section of chapter 8, and you should have a healthy, natural looking tan you've applied with no specialist equipment whatsoever.

My thanks go to Catherine at Fresh Indulgence for her input for this section.

8

What does a bad spray tan look like?

A bad spray tan can be the result of either technician or client, or even both. It really does depend on the experience of the tanning technician applying the tan, whether the correct tan tone percentage chosen and whether the client has followed the before care advice correctly.

You need to impress upon your clients that the preparation before the tan is **just as** important as the spray tan application itself. Discuss the look your client wants to achieve and choose the tan tone percentage together.

You can never ask a client too many questions about the look they want from their spray tan. It's not being nosey, it's about getting the right result, as your choice of colour may be different to theirs. Make sure you get it right for *them*, or they may never return to you.

The most common spray tan tone solutions to use are 8% (light) 10% (medium) and 12% (dark). If you are in any doubt as to which tan tone to apply to your client, play it safe and choose your lightest to medium colour and explain your reasoning to your client.

Once you see a bad spray tan, you never forget it. It's often down to poor application; the typical signs of which include telltale signs on the feet and hands, banding, patching or a badly chosen colour. A bad spray tan will often put a client off for good, and that's unfortunate, because they've probably seen many good spray tans without even realising it.

Make sure you don't overdo the application…you're not spraying a car. Make sure you recommend a spray tan colour tone percentage that will suit your client, unless they state they want a very dark spray tan (you may want to record this was not your chosen tan tone percentage on your consultation form). Choose a good product that you've tried and tested yourself at least half a dozen times with no orange undertone and perfect your technique before you take on any paying clients.

What should a good spray tan look like? Again this is down to the individual, but for most you shouldn't be able to distinguish a spray tan from a natural sun-kissed look, depending on the client's natural colour skin tone. By using a lighter spray tan tone, typically 8% on a fair skinned person, you actually promote the client's features; hair, make-up and clothes. That makes a light tone a good choice for brides and proms.

When you look at a darker spray tanned person, it's the tan you remember, and if it's been badly applied, for all the wrong reasons. This over-tanned look can ruin a good look; especially bad if your client's going to a lot of trouble for a special occasion, or has spent money on other grooming treatments and an outfit.

If, on the other hand the wearer of a spray tan is a dancer or entering a muscle competition then the extra, dark fake tanned look will be far more fitting.

So there is an opinion and reason for all spray tan tones, just choose the right one **with** your client to get the perfect finish.

Patchy and faded spray tans

Patchy spray tans do happen, so it's important that your clients aren't on the receiving end.

If your client is very pale skinned and you apply the darkest spray tan, then the inevitable fading process will be uneven, resulting in patches. The difference between natural skin colour and the spray tan tone used will be significant, and that's likely to mean an unhappy client.

Applying a moisturiser to the body too soon before the spray tan is applied can also cause patching as it sometimes acts as a barrier. Some parts of the body will absorb the moisturiser quickly and other parts of the body may take longer, so the best bet is always to moisturise well the evening before a spray tan, concentrating on the very dry areas of elbows, knees, feet and hands. This will give plenty of time for the moisturising lotion to be absorbed evenly. Make sure you recommend an oil-free moisturiser.

Products that contain alpha hydroxy acids (AHA) can seriously interfere with a spray tan, causing patching and fading. Products containing AHAs are usually marketed for smoothing fine lines and surface wrinkles, improving skin texture and tone, unblocking and cleansing pores, and improving skin condition in general. You'll mostly find them in face and neck products, but occasionally in body creams and soaps.

Sometimes AHAs are used in cosmetics to adjust the pH (the degree of acidity or alkalinity) value. AHA-containing products cause exfoliation, or shedding of the surface skin. The extent of exfoliation depends on the type and concentration of the AHA, its pH, and other ingredients in the product.

Anti-acne products tend to make the face dry out and even peel, so these products can cause premature fading and uneven patching, as can facial toners with a high content of alcohol.

Sodium lauryl sulfate (SLS) is used in low concentrations in toothpastes, shampoos, shower gels and shaving foams. It's an important component in bubble bath formulations for its thickening effect and ability to create lather. Products containing SLS may fade a spray tan prematurely.

Facial hair bleachers will strip the spray tan on the face and products with Retina-A and facial cleansers that contain oil will fade and make the spray tan patch. This can be very noticeable around the mouth and nose area.

Hands and feet tend to patch regardless of which tan tone percentage is used. Hands are washed more often for hygiene reasons throughout the day and feet are constantly rubbing in a shoe and tend to sweat, which will cause a spray tan to rub off. These areas are very noticeable so make sure your client is aware of the premature patching and how much more noticeable it will be should they choose a very dark spray tan.

Patching and fading can also happen on the hips and waist. The hips and waist often rub in tight clothes throughout a normal day, causing a spray tan to dry out and leave patches, which should also be discussed with the client.

Propylene glycol is used in moisturisers, medicines, cosmetics, food, toothpaste, shampoo, mouthwash, and hair care and as a carrier in fragrance oils. It's an ingredient in massage oils and hand sanitisers, antibacterial lotions, and saline solutions and can be present in tanning solutions. In body products it can wear at the spray tan a little quicker. Exposure to mists may cause eye irritation, as well as upper respiratory tract irritation. Inhalation of the propylene glycol vapours appears to present no significant hazard in ordinary applications. However, inhalation of propylene glycol mists could be irritating to **some** individuals, so it's best to avoid inhalation wherever possible. You may want to **do your own research** on this product, as evidence and opinion is mixed.

Perfumes and deodorants may cause patching as they can act as a barrier, so make sure you tell your client to be free of these and all other cosmetics. Insect repellent sprays, when sprayed directly onto the skin, can remove and cause a spray tan to fade and patch.

Surgical tape, plasters and bandages will strip the spray tan, causing patching, and shaving with a blunt blade can sometimes causing stripes on a spray tanned body.

Tell your client not to rub or scratch their spray tan, especially when it has just been applied, as this will cause patches or stripes when the spray tan develops. The client must not exfoliate once the spray tan has been applied or use a harsh loofah or rough wash mitt. Bathing needs to be kept short and the water not too hot, to reduce fading. Pat the body dry with a towel after a shower and do **not** rub.

Certain parts of our bodies, such as the back, chest and face, can be extra oily, acting as a barrier to the solution. Clients should be advised to exfoliate these areas thoroughly and avoid using moisturisers.

There are 'prep sprays' on the market. It's claimed that when sprayed onto the skin they prevent patchy and faded tans by removing oils, make-up, deodorant and sweat residue while enabling optimal penetration of spray tanning solutions. It may be worth your while buying and testing these sprays on yourself to see if they work before you start applying these to your clients'. Make sure you take a close look at the ingredients so that you don't cause any allergic reactions.

It's worth noting that anti-ageing products, facial bleaches and most products used to speed up skin renewal can also cause skin blotching, making it difficult to determine any reaction to a spray tan.

The following are some commonly used products that can lighten, fade, patch or make a spray tan blotchy:

- Anti-ageing products that claim to renew, refresh or exfoliate the skin

- Hair-inhibiting lotions

- Alpha hydroxy acids (AHAs), glycolic, tartaric, lactic, malic and citric acids

- Beta hydroxy acids (BHAs), also referred to as salicylic acids

- Retinol-A type products (Retin-A, Renovate, Tazorac, and Trefinoin)

- Toners containing witch hazel or alcohol

- Anti-acne products that exfoliate the skin; accutane or salicylic acid

- Make-up remover, facial cleaning products or oils used to remove make-up

- Soap bars, especially deodorant or antibacterial varieties

- Sugar soaps

- Plaster aids or adhesive tape

- Facial masks

- Exfoliating scrubs

- Sodium lauryl sulfate (SLS)

- Adhesive facial strips

- Curel lotion

- Wax hair removal

- Propylene glycol

- Depilatory hair removal products

- Bug spray, when sprayed directly onto the skin. Clients should spray clothing if the product must be used.

You'll benefit from doing your own research into these products.

What does a bad spray tan look like?

9

Sammy's Scrub
share it with your clients

This homemade scrub may help you extend your airbrush spray tan a little longer. It's very cheap to produce and extremely easy to apply. Why not share Sammy's Scrub with your clients?

Things you'll need: sea salt or beach sand; your favourite shower gel; some moisturising lotion.

- Step 1: The secret to extending your tan is exfoliation - this is an absolute must! First you'll need to make your exfoliant. Get a bottle of your favourite shower gel. Make sure it is **oil-free**. You cannot use sugar scrubs or similar because they'll actually reduce the life of your airbrush tan.

- Step 2: Add three tablespoons of beach sand or children's sand pit sand (if you haven't got easy access to sand then use sea salt instead, usually available at your local supermarket) and shake well.

- Step 3: Jump in the shower and use your freshly made body scrub. I like to use it for at least two days in a row before I know I'm going to apply a spray tan, but I don't have sensitive skin and I always wash with a pH-balancing soap. Scrub your body thoroughly, paying extra attention to your knees, elbows, feet and hands, where spray tan will typically cling. Always moisturise after exfoliating, but **not** on the day of your spray tan unless you have *really* dry skin, in which case you should do it at least four hours before.

- Step 4: On the day you are going to have your airbrush spray tan applied, **do not** apply any oil-based or high alcohol lotions, deodorants, body sprays, perfumes or anti-aging products as they may react with your tan.

- Step 5: Get spray tanned as directed by your salon or mobile tanning technician. Let your tan stay on your body overnight if you can to allow it time to develop fully. If this is not possible, make sure it's left on at least 12 hours or as advised by your technician.

- Step 6: Now that you've set a perfect base for your tan, you must take care of it. Hydrate! Drink plenty of water and put moisturising lotion on your skin at least once a day, twice if you can. Moisturising should first take place following your first shower post-tan, preferably the next day. Use oil and alcohol-free lotion if possible to avoid premature wearing of the tan.

Remember: the spray tan is only on the top layer of your skin. As your skin naturally sheds cells daily, you lose your tan. You cannot stop this process, but you **can** slow the process down. Exfoliating beforehand removes all our dead layers of skin, and frequent hydration keeps the living cells going for that little bit longer, leading to a longer-lasting tan.

N.B: If you have sensitive skin, always seek your GP's advice on a body scrub or any new and unfamiliar product that might irritate your delicate condition further.

It's a great idea to create a leaflet along these lines to distribute to your clients.

10

Some frequently asked questions

Q: How long should my spray tan last me?

A: It all depends on how well you've prepared your skin, how well you look after it post-application, and of course on your skin type. The average is anywhere between 5 and 10 days, but if you have a spray tan fairly regularly you'll find that your skin retains colour a little longer as it becomes used to the solution.

Q: Will the spray tanning solution harm my eyes?

A: While the solution is apparently not harmful to the eyes, you should always keep your eyes closed while your face and upper body are being sprayed. DHA is Food and Drug Administration (FDA) approved for external application but is not deemed safe for application to lips, mucous membranes or if inhaled. This does not mean it is poisonous, it means that testing has not established what effects it has other than on the skin, so make sure not to let the spray tan solution get inside the mouth, genital area, eyes or nose. The FDA recommends wearing protective eye goggles and even nose plugs as a precaution.

Q: Will a spray tan protect me from being sunburnt?

A: Not at all - any time you go out in the sun for sustained periods you should apply approved sun protection.

We automatically think that when we have had a spray tan applied, since our skin is now a lovely brown we don't need to wear sun protection...this is very wrong. Spray tan solutions do not have any sun factor protection in them at all and if they did, we would need to be spraying ourselves with the spray tanning solution every couple of hours to protect ourselves while sunbathing, just as we have to apply our sun screens every couple of hours. When sunbathing you need to protect yourself with a sun screen; preferably one with no oil, as the oil will remove your tan.

Tanning enhancers are often used in the evening as a moisturiser after a spray tan application, to keep the spray tan topped up, and selling these can help increase your profits.

Q: I've had a bad experience with spray tanning before – does this mean my skin is unsuitable?

A: Not at all. The quality of a spray tan depends on a number of things, not least the type and quality of the solution itself and of course the skill of the tanning technician.

People often don't realise how important their skin condition is: did you follow the before advice given before the spray tan and did you use a moisturiser?

Were you on medication (including antibiotics and chemotherapy medication)?

Even your monthly period and breast-feeding can affect a spray tan because your skin is extra sensitive due to hormonal changes.

It's worth trying a different solution or even technician, but at the very least make sure you exfoliate and make follow the before and aftercare advice your technician gives you. Go for a light tan next time around. Once in a while someone does find that they simply don't take the tan, but the odds are that with a few changes you'll be just the colour you want to be.

Q: Why did my last spray tan come out differently to the previous one, even though it was performed in the same salon using the same solution?

A: If all other elements of application were the same, it's likely that your skin is behind the difference. The reality is that skin condition varies depending on the weather, your menstrual cycle, diet, stress and of course any medication you may be taking.

The exception to this rule is when the solution has passed its shelf life or wasn't stored properly, causing the DHA to deteriorate. To be able to answer this question honestly and helpfully, always use in-date products and always take care of them.

Q: Can I go swimming after receiving a spray tan?

A: Wait overnight for your spray tan to develop. Chlorinated water can bleach your tan, so I suggest you avoid using a swimming pool. The sea doesn't contain chlorine of course, but if you must take a dip keep it brief – salt can help in exfoliation and can have a drying effect on skin, so the longer you're exposed to saltwater, the faster you'll lose your tan.

Q: Is it OK to have a spray tan when you're under 18 years old?

A: Yes it is. However, I recommend the signature and presence of the parent or guardian for those under the age of 18.

Recommending that they are clothed in their full underwear unless the parent is present is just a precaution to protect you, the technician.

Q: Will a spray tan get rid of my cellulite?

A: A spray tan will not get rid of cellulite but it will help disguise it, just as it will help disguise spider veins.

Q: How brown will I go with a spray tan?

A: Everybody's skin is different, and so each person develops their own colour - the tan tone percentage chosen for the spray tan plays a part too. Some clients go a dark brown while others may get a much subtler colour. Regular sessions can help the skin to acclimatise to receiving tanning solution, and over a fairly short space of time a darker colour can be achieved.

Q: I have just had Botox - will this affect my spray tan?

A: If you have just been administered Botox and/or fillers you should wait at least 48 hours before you receive a spray tan.

A spray tan should not affect these treatments, but the skin may be a little sensitive, so check with a qualified and experienced medical professional how long they recommend you should wait.

Q: Can I have sex after a spray tan?

A: Not immediately, since if you sweat, your tan will run and rub off, causing patching when it has developed. If your spray tan contains a bronzer, it will rub onto your partner and sadly that doesn't mean two tans for the price of one, the result will be patches everywhere. You will also mark your bedding. If your spray tan was a clear solution rather than containing bronzer, wait its allocated developing time before getting into bed for anything more strenuous than sleeping. If the solution contained a bronzer, wait the allocated developing time, have a shower and then carry on.

Q: If I have very fair skin that doesn't tan, will a spray tan work for me?

A: Absolutely – after all spray tanning was invented to solve this very problem.

Q: Even though we've had the same tanning solution, my friend and I are completely different colours – I'm an unnatural orange colour. Why is this?

A: You and your friend share the same tanning solution, but not the same skin type. Your best options are to try a different product or a spray tan tone percentage that's better suited to your skin type.

Q: If I have hair on my legs or arms will the tan be even?

A: Hair is not too much of a problem but the technician may have to apply your spray tan lighter than normal, depending on the amount of hair on your body and so the process may take a little longer. At the end of your spray tan you may notice tiny droplets of solution on the hair on your body, but just wiping very gently with tissue or blowing gently with a hairdryer will remove any excess.

Q: Does the spray tanning solution smell bad, like the self-tanning solutions you can buy in the shops?

A: It varies from product to product, so some will, but others have a very pleasant smell. Your best bet is to ask for a particular 'flavour' - cherry, coconut, chocolate and almond are just a few of the scents available. Either way, the smell will disappear when you take your first shower.

Q: Can I use normal soap after a spray tan?

A: It's recommended you use soap with a pH balance of 5.5 or lower as higher pH soaps, for example antibacterial and deodorant soaps, could fade your spray tan quicker.

Our skin is naturally slightly acidic, with a pH of around 5.5. Unfortunately, many skin treatments, and soaps in particular, are alkaline; meaning they'll raise your skin's pH above its natural levels, causing the spray tan to fade quicker.

Q: My chest and neck are peeling – why?

A: There could be many reasons for this (see patchy and faded tans), but the simplest answer could just be that peeling is a result of perfumes or moisturisers applied either before or after the spray tanning session. Some perfumes are absorbed deeply enough to resist scrubbing and showering, and your particular skin type may require more frequent or thorough preparatory exfoliation.

Q: Is the spray tanning solution safe?

A: Yes, all of the components in spray tanning solution are approved by the Food and Drug Administration (FDA) and have been used in food and cosmetics for over 30 years.

A technician should be able to provide the list of ingredients of the chosen spray tanning solution if the client states they have allergies or sensitive skin. If the client has sensitive skin or allergies to any of those products used in the chosen tanning solution, their skin may also react when applied.

Q: How soon after the spray tan can I shower?

A: The most common recommended developing time for a spray tan on is overnight. However, some technicians would say you can leave just 5 hours before you shower. Find out the recommended time from the supplier or manufacturer of the product used, as all products are different.

Using the spray tanning solutions on yourself will give you real experience on the showering process to pass onto your clients, and that's more meaningful than anything else. If you spray tanned your client with a clear solution then you might choose to go to bed without showering and wake up brown...but if the solution contained a bronzer, there is the risk of marking or staining the bed sheets. Advise your clients to sleep on old bedding as a precaution; nylon and silk in particular are prone to staining.

Q: I am on antibiotics; will this affect my spray tan?

A: It may do, as some medications can cause a different skin colour reaction to spray tanning.

Q: Will a spray tan hide my stretch marks?

A: A spray tan will help to disguise stretch marks and scarring, but scarred skin sometimes does not absorb the solution as well as normal skin.

Q: Will a spray tan dry out my skin?

A: Yes it may do if the tanning solution contains high amounts of alcohol. Most tanning solutions have a minimal amount of pure alcohol or drying preservative, but it's an active ingredient that helps the solution to dry when applied to the skin. You can help prevent the skin from drying out further through regular moisturising once or twice a day. Higher alcohol solutions can benefit a client who tends to have greasier natural skin.

Q: Will my contact lenses be ok worn for a spray tan?

A: Contact lenses should be removed, as the solution will be more likely to irritate the eyes if it has contact with the lenses.

Q: I am diabetic, is spray tanning OK for me?

A: DHA is a chemical derived from glycerine and was first used in the treatment of diabetes, as some diabetics are better able to tolerate DHA than glucose in their treatment! So basically, yes you can have an airbrush spray tan.

This decision is down to the technician to decide if they feel the spray tan should be applied to a diabetic.

Q: Can I spray tan if I am pregnant?

A: Spray tanning in pregnancy is presumed safe and no problems have been reported, however the first trimester of pregnancy is a critical time, so for this time a spray tan should be avoided.

The following six months of pregnancy is going to be down to the discretion of the technician and if a client insists the spray tan goes ahead you will need written permission from the client's doctor. Make sure you record all details on the consultation form and keep a copy of the GP's letter. Hormones are very high in pregnancy so it's quite possible that the spray tan will be affected and it may be wisest to avoid a spray tan altogether.

Q: Will a massage affect my tan?

A: Yes, massaging your spray tanned skin, especially using massage oils, will prematurely take your spray tan off. If massage is a treatment you have regularly, wait a week after your spray tan application. At this point the tan will be beginning to fade anyway.

Q: I am a mature lady; can I have a spray tan?

A: Sure you can, but exfoliation and moisturising is even more important for a mature client. The skin tends to be thinner and dryer and this can cause the same problems as spray tanning a client with noticeably dry skin.

The tanning solution may develop a little darker so bear in mind that the DHA tan tone percentage needs to be the lighter choice for the client.

Q: What if I have a bald spot on my head?

A: You can have your scalp spray tanned, although a lighter colour may need to be used to avoid affecting the natural colour of your hair.

The head can be spray tanned, but high bronzing agents in solutions may need to be avoided on bleached, fair or greying hair as it may colour this type hair. A spray tanning solution with no bronzer can be used on the head but remember that if the body is sprayed with a bronzing solution there'll be noticeable colour on the body but not on the head until the tan develops! Best practice would be to use the same solution all over.

Q: Will a spray tan affect the colour of my eyelashes and eyebrows?

A: Yes, it can if your eyelashes and eyebrows are fair, tinted or bleached and the spray tanning solution used has a high tan tone percentage. Using a barrier cream on the eyebrows and eye pads on the eyelids helps avoid this problem. Mascara on the lashes can help protect them.

Q: Will the rain affect my spray tan?

A: Yes, it will if the spray tan has just been applied, so cover up and prepare for rain by taking an umbrella with you just in case. If the spray tan has been on the skin for its recommended developing time, the rain will not affect a spray tan unless you haven't washed off the bronzing agent, in which case you may get rain marks until it is washed off.

Q: Will a spray tan harm my tattoos?

A: No, spray tanning solutions will not harm a tattoo, but the light ink tones on your tattoo, eg yellows and whites, can slightly darken in colour and look slightly faded with a spray tan applied. This **is** only temporary, until your tan has worn off. New tattoos should **not** have a spray tan applied until they are fully healed.

11
Consultation forms

A consultation form is an absolute must when it comes to airbrush spray tanning. Everybody should keep a record of every client's detailed answers for their own protection. If you're unsure about an answer that's given, then my best advice would be not to spray tan that client until you've been given a firm and clear response, or in some cases had a doctor's letter produced. Verbal confirmation is **not** enough.

Filling out a consultation form does take a little time, but it's time worth taking. All the information you collect from the client is vital to choosing the correct solution and giving the correct before and aftercare advice. Get to know skin types. Oily, dry, combination and normal skin are all very different and your chosen solution may adversely affect the end result of a spray tan if your advice was inaccurate.

You may find it simplest to send out a consultation form in advance, via email or post, to save some time.

The form is there to protect you and your client. It demonstrates professionalism and may even jog a client's memory regarding a skin condition or illness. So you can never ask too many questions. Reassure your client that all information collected will remain in strict confidence and not be passed to any third party. And mean it too; this is a serious responsibility.

I always fill out two consultation forms per client with carbon paper in between. Some might think this overly cautious, but by giving a client a copy as well as keeping one for my own records, there's no room for argument or misinterpretation. I keep the top copy in an A4 folder for future visits and give the client the under copy.

Remember: your insurance cover could become invalid if a consultation form is not filled in.

Here's a list of details you should consider including on your form:

- Client's name

- Client's date of birth

- Home address, phone number and email address

- Which spray tan solution you used

- Which tan tone percentage was used

- The date the spray tan was applied

- Client's skin type and hair colour

- Any allergies, sensitive skin or breathing conditions such as asthma

- Any skin conditions, such as eczema, psoriasis, ringworm, warts, verrucas or impetigo

- Any cuts, rashes, acne or scars

- Any medical conditions such as diabetes

- Whether the client is currently on any medication

- Whether the client has had any facial enhancements such as Botox or fillers

- Whether they client uses AHA (skin renewal products)

- Do they have tattoos or body piercings? If so, how recent are they?

- Is the client pregnant or breast-feeding?

- Has any alcohol been consumed during the previous 24 hours?

- Does the client wear contact lenses?

- Check whether the client has exfoliated and followed all before-care advice

- Ask whether the client has shaved or waxed in the previous 24 hours

- Find out if the client has used self-tan products before and whether there has ever been a reaction

- Ask if the client is wearing any moisturiser, deodorants, perfume or make-up

- Request confirmation that the client has removed all jewellery

- Request confirmation that an extractor unit was used during the treatment

- Include that all-important disclaimer and signature box at the bottom of the consultation form.

On the opposite page you'll find an example demonstrating how you can fit the minimum information you should be gathering, including the disclaimer, onto an A4 piece of paper.

Client Consultation Card

Please complete all answers below with **yes** or **no**. If answering **yes**, please provide all relevant details.

Date: _____

Product used today _____ Tan tone % _____

Name: _____

Address: _____

Postcode: _____ Home phone: _____

Email:_____

Mobile: _____DOB: ____/ ____/ ____ M / F (delete as applicable)

Skin type: Dry? _____ Oily? _____ Normal? _____ Combination? _____ Are you pregnant? _____

Have you any allergies or suffer from asthma? _____

Do you use any AHA products for skin renewal,
eg smoothing wrinkles, improving skin condition?_____

Are you on any medication? _____ Have you consumed alcohol in the last 24 hrs? _____

Do you have any open cuts, rashes, acne, or recent operation scars? _____

Do you suffer from any skin disorders? _____ Are they infectious? _____

Eczema? _____ Psoriasis?_____ Ringworm? _____

Warts? _____ _____Verrucas?_____ Impetigo? _____

Have you any new tattoos or body piercing? _____ If yes, how recently?_____

Are you breast-feeding? _____ _____ Are you diabetic? _____

Do you have sensitive, broken or cracked skin? _____

Have you used any self-tan products before? _____ _____Did you ever have a reaction? _____

Do you wear contact lenses? _____ Do you have bleached or coloured hair? _____

Have you exfoliated? _____ Were you advised to exfoliate?_____

Are you wearing any moisturisers, perfume, deodorant or make-up? _____

Have you shaved or waxed within the last 24 hours? _____

Have you removed all jewellery? _____

Any recent facial enhancements eg Botox, fillers? _____

Was an extractor unit/fan used today on your visit? _____

Disclaimer: I declare that all the above information is correct and I have no medical condition that may affect or induce a harmful reaction from a spray tan.

I know of no reason therefore why I shouldn't receive a spray tan.

*Customer signature: _____ Date: _____
(Parent if under 18 years old)

*Therapist signature: _____ Date:_____

12
Aftercare

Good aftercare is vital to maintaining a spray tan for as long as possible.

- Instruct the client not to bathe or shower for at least 12 hours and to leave the spray tan on overnight if possible - 24 hours for the best results. This gives the spray tan plenty of time to fully develop into the skin.

- Tell your client that the chlorine in swimming water will strip their spray tan.

- Tell your client vigorous exercise will also affect their spray tan, with all the inevitable sweating and the rubbing of clothes against skin. This applies particularly to when the spray tan is first applied, but also the duration of the spray tan on the body. This will cause the spray tan to patch and fade.

- Advise the client to moisturise their body fully the next day, after their first light shower, and regularly thereafter to prevent the skin from drying out. Using a suitable moisturiser will increase the length of time the spray tan lasts, slowing down the skin shedding process.

- Advise the client to wear loose clothing after the tanning application and to cover leather upholstery with a towel if any skin is bare.

- Advise clients to use sun cream and/or sun block if going in the sun, as spray tan solutions do not contain any sun protection.

- Never use any moisturisers or sun-creams that have oil or high alcohol content, as this will wear the spray tan off prematurely.

- Give every client an aftercare leaflet to take away with them with every possible tip to maintain their spray tan. The next chapter provides you with some guidance on creating the most helpful and informative aftercare leaflets for your clients.

Aftercare

13
Aftercare leaflets

You should always give your client an aftercare leaflet. An aftercare leaflet tells your client how to maintain their spray tan once it has been applied to ensure the maximum lasting effect.

Below are two examples you can use to help design your own.

Making the most of your spray tan

Straight after your treatment

We recommend that you:

- Leave your spray tan for at least 12 hours, overnight if possible and 24 hours ideally, before showering or taking a bath. This gives your tan a chance to fully develop.

- Avoid wearing socks or shoes after your tanning session as sweating can inhibit the development of your tan. Sandals or flip-flops are a good choice.

- Avoid applying moisturiser, deodorant or perfume as this could react with your tan; wait till after your first shower.

- Avoid wearing tight clothing for at least 7 hours.

- All swimming, showering and vigorous exercise must be avoided for at least 7 hours as this can inhibit the development of your tan.

- Don't sit on light-coloured leather or fabrics until you've showered or taken a bath as the color guide in the spray tan may transfer and cause discolouration.

- Don't shave until 24 hours after your treatment. Ideally you should shave before your spray tan; the longer shaving can be left once the tan has been applied the better, as shaving wears at the tan.

Remember: don't panic if you see colour in your shower or bath water. This is just the colour guide and washing it off will reveal your fantastic tan beneath.

Making the most of your spray tan

Maintaining your spray tan

We recommend that you:

- Moisturise regularly; twice daily if you can. Hydrated skin is essential in maintaining a longer life to your tan.

- Avoid long hot baths and showers as they tend to speed up exfoliation.

- Pat your skin dry after a bath or shower. Rubbing your skin may take off your tan.

- Avoid swimming pools with chlorine, as these will strip your tan.

- If bathing in seawater, keep swims short, as this will strip your tan.

- Take care when exercising; as sweating may cause your tan to fade unevenly.

Note: moisturising lotions containing alpha hydroxy acids (AHA) are used to increase exfoliation, so using them will accelerate the fading process of your tan.

14
Training

If you're interested in pursuing a career in spray tanning, even if you've recently undertaken a course with a view, a number of questions may have occurred to you.

- If you're qualified, how well have you been trained?

- Did you leave your training school confident in your ability to sell and apply a professional spray tan?

- Is the training school closest to you the one you should opt for?

- Do you need the latest expensive equipment?

Regardless of how much you pay, there's no guarantee of a perfect end result. Poor applications earn you nothing more than a bad reputation and no clientele. There are many points to take on board and research is key.

Find out what your spray tanning course will cover before you hand over your fee and make sure that on completion of the course you'll receive a certificate that's recognised by reputable insurance companies – I can't stress the importance of this too strongly.

In the event of a claim being made against you, you'll need to produce your qualifying certificate and may even be asked to show the course syllabus handed out on your training day.

Some points you should consider when choosing a spray tanning course are:

- Health, safety and hygiene

- Risk assessments

- Professional ethics

- Course syllabus

- Recognised insurable certificate

- The operation of the airbrush and compressor

- Looking after your equipment

- How to apply the perfect tan with clear instructions on how to position your client

- Correction of mistakes

- Record keeping

- Before and aftercare

- Contraindications to the treatment

- Skin diseases

- Allergies

- Understanding of DHA solutions

- Practical spray tan to models

- Aftercare form provided to get you started

- Consultation form provided to get you started

- Troubleshooting

- Helpline, even after you've paid your fees.

15
Organising your workspace

As with all salon and mobile practice, it's important that you keep a well-organised and tidy workplace; you'll reduce the risk of accidents and maintain a professional image.

Run all cables safely and don't overload sockets or extension leads.

Keep all products and electrical equipment out of the reach of any customers' children.

Make sure your airbrush is always clean and in good working order.

Make sure your colour feeder bottle is full of solution before you start work and securely attached to your airbrush gun to avoid a spillage.

Make sure you have a spare feeder bottle with an adequate amount of water, in case you need to clean your airbrush during a spray tan application. Prepare a feeder bottle with an adequate amount of cleaning fluid to blow through your airbrush gun, before if needed, but always after your spray tan application.

Make sure you have a roll of paper towel or tissues:

- For protecting clothes if you are doing a partial tan

- For blotting if you get a run

- For starting your client's tan: spraying firstly onto tissue before continuing to apply the spray tan solution to the skin.

Always put yourself in your client's shoes: would **you** want to be kept standing around in your underwear while a stranger faffs around? No. So get all your equipment and accessories ready before asking your client to undress.

16
Insurance

Insurance is essential as mistakes do happen. You might think it'll never happen to you, but you're being naïve if you think you'll never come across a client you can never ever please.

Don't take the risk of leaving your insurance to the last minute, or think "I will see how things go"…it takes just one person to ruin you professionally and financially. With the many horror stories I've heard over the years, it's just not worth taking the chance.

One year's insurance will set you back around £60-£100 depending on your exact needs. When you divide it into a daily rate, a £100 premium works out at just 27p per day…so you really are looking at just pennies to protect your livelihood.

The most commonplace accidents include knocking solution bottles over, which then damage carpets and floors, and the breakage of lights and chinaware. Obvious though it may sound, the only way to avoid accidents is be extra careful. Secure your solution bottles and set up your equipment in a safe place to avoid breakages.

From time to time a client will faint during a spray tan. Not, I hasten to add, as a direct consequence of the tanning application itself. It's pretty alarming if it happens, and if you're lucky you'll catch your client and stop him or her smashing head or teeth on the floor. You may not be at fault, but it's yet another example of the value of professional indemnity insurance.

This funky chicken dance is usually performed by younger girls who've been out the night before, taken on a bellyful of alcohol, and are dehydrated. Of course you're not really in a position to judge a client's situation at a glance, so you could address this issue on your consultation form. If they've been painting the town red the night before, offering a glass of water before their spray tan may just save you a load of grief.

If your client will be standing for a long period I'd always advise them **not** to lock their knees, as a looser stance will help the blood flow run freely around the body. Standing with knees slightly bent doesn't affect the application of a spray tan and might just help avoid some future claims against your insurance. Other useful tricks include wiggling toes to keep the blood circulation going and building up and swallowing saliva repeatedly.

My advice would be to arrange your insurance as soon as you pass your spray tanning course.

17
Health and safety

Many local councils set out their own requirements for the safe operation of spray tanning businesses. Check your area to ensure you comply with all regulations and recommendations.

I've dealt with many health and safety concerns during the course of this book, but the checklist below highlights the key issues you should look into, whether you're working as a mobile technician or running a salon.

Checklist

- COSHH (Control of Substances Hazardous to Health)
  Obtain Material Safety Data Sheets for the tanning product from the supplier or manufacturer. Salons should assess the safety of the product, in the form of a COSHH appraisal and identify any potential ingredients likely to cause allergic reactions or respiratory problems.
  Consider also:

  - Safe and suitable product storage

  - Labelling and ingredients; check active ingredient dihydroxyacetone.

  - Knowledge of potential risks/health effects

  - Client health history, including allergies, medical conditions and skin patch tests. Clients suffering with asthma for instance are advised by the manufacturer to consult their GP before using some spray products.

- Ventilation requirements: ensure that filters and extraction systems are maintained on a regular basis to ensure optimum efficiency. Manual tanning systems technicians should ensure a specific site assessment is carried out to ensure sufficient and adequate ventilation. Manufacturers' instructions will provide guidance, but some reports suggest that swallowing some tanning products may cause nausea, vomiting, gastrointestinal irritation and diarrhoea. Clients should be appropriately warned.

- Training of staff: all staff should be given appropriate information, instruction and training on the use of the tanning equipment and associated products. Operating manuals should be accessible to all staff.

- Upper limb disorders. The repetitive nature of manual spray tan application could lead to RSI (repetitive strain injury) and require the technician to take up awkward postures. Staff training and adequate workspace is essential to safe working.

- Manual handling: Especially relevant for the 23kg drums used in tanning booths

- PPE: personal protective equipment. Where gloves and masks are used, particularly with the manual spray system, protective equipment must be of the approved type and replaced as required.

- Slips and trips: a potential hazard given that the liquid is sprayed as a fine mist which may settle on the floor. The use of anti-slip matting and regular cleaning is vital.

- Air compressor: there are explosion/noise risks associated with compressors. Spray booth compressors warrant a written scheme of examination. All compressors must comply with the Pressure Systems Safety Regulations 2000.

- Electrical safety checks. Electric shock is also a potential hazard with automated booths, which are operated from a 240v supply. The equipment maintenance involves accessing the service compartment, which houses the electrical circuitry. Any staff responsible for this kind of duty must be competently trained to reduce the risk of electric shock.

- Legionella bacteria checks. The water supply for automatic spray booths in particular provides ideal breeding conditions for Legionella bacteria. Salon owners are advised to carry out a risk assessment to identify and assess potential sources of exposure.

- Waste disposal: waste generated with these systems is classed as trade effluent and requires a trade effluent licence from the local water authority.

Legislative requirements for salon operatives

- *The Pressure Systems Safety Regulations 2000*

- *The Health and Safety at Work etc Act 1974*

- *Control of Substances Hazardous to Health Regulations 2002*

- *The Work Place Health Safety and Welfare Regulations 1992*

- *The Management of Health and Safety at Work Regulations 1999*

It's worth keeping up to date with the latest health and safety regulations and rulings at: www.hse.gov.uk, the government-run Health and Safety Executive website.

New business owners may also find www.hsadviser.co.uk/hsa_starterpack a useful port of call. I'd recommend checking in with one or both of these websites at least every six months.

You can get also get a full health and safety pack from the HABIA website: www.habia.org. HABIA is the government-appointed standards body for the beauty industry and in addition to health and safety advice, their website is a great place to go to read up on training, careers, industry events and the latest research and statistics.

On the 8th April 2011 the sunbed Regulations Act 2010 came in to force. Under new regulations, under 18s are now banned from using sunbeds at: leisure centres, beauty salons, gyms, hotels and other premises.

Its now illegal to offer under 18s the use of sunbeds - fail to comply with these regulations and allow the under 18s to use sunbeds and you could face a huge fine!

My thanks go to Michael Duck, environmental health officer at Fylde Borough Council, in compiling this checklist.

18
Contraindications

Contraindications are warnings about the risks of proceeding with some kind of treatment. Here I'm going to list some of the skin conditions and health concerns you should be looking out for. All information should be recorded on the consultation form.

❑ Do not spray tan clients if they have warts, athlete's foot, impetigo, herpes, ringworm, verrucas, scabies or any other contagious or infectious skin condition. Do your research on contagious infections so you know what to look out for, as a client may have answered 'no' to the question asked because they don't know they have them. A spray tan could irritate these conditions or, worse still, you yourself may end up with the condition.

❑ You should not spray tan women in the first three months of pregnancy. No harmful effects have ever been reported as far as I am aware, but I think it's too risky. The body's hormones fluctuate when you are pregnant and not only may there be an allergic reaction, but the colour tone may develop very differently. If your client insists on having a spray tan and you want to provide it, then you will need their doctor's written permission. Make a copy of the letter and attach it to the consultation form. A far safer form of professional protection would be not to perform the treatment however; it's better to be safe than sorry.

❑ If a client's skin is broken, bruised, cracked or inflamed, whether from psoriasis, eczema, open acne, rashes, burns, boils, open wounds, or cuts and abrasions, then you should not spray tan the client. Again, the solution could cause irritation and exacerbate the condition. If the client's skin is very dry but intact, and you gave your client all the right advice about preparing for the treatment, then make sure you spray the solution very lightly over any dry areas. A barrier cream or moisturiser can be applied to very dry knees, elbows, feet and hands.

❑ If a client has sunburn it's best to avoid spray tanning. Sunburn displays redness and sensitivity of the skin first, which is followed by blistering and peeling. The cells of the outer layer of the skin are badly injured, and the sweat glands become swollen and largely non-functional. Sunburn is classed as a first-degree burn and while it injures only the epidermis and heals without leaving scars, the spray tan solution may irritate or cause a reaction.

❑ Many spray tanning technicians don't realise that some spray tanning solutions contain almond extract or walnut extract, so a client with a nut allergy could very easily suffer an allergic reaction. Always get a breakdown of all ingredients used in each of your tanning solutions, so you know which solution to avoid if the client suffers any allergies. This question should **always** be on your consultation form and filled in accordingly.

❑ People can get hives for lots of different reasons. While the cause is often unknown, one frequent reason is an allergic reaction. Common allergic triggers include certain foods, like milk, shellfish, berries and nuts, medications such as antibiotics, and insect stings or bites.

❑ The active ingredient in spray tanning solution is dihydroxyacetone (DHA). There is a small chance that your client might be allergic to this. A client who already has sensitive skin and tends to react to different types of lotions, foods, plants and chemicals will probably react to the spray tan solution, so always perform a patch test first.

❑ Clients who suffer from severe asthma or other breathing difficulties could encounter major problems because of spray tan overspray. Make sure the question is asked on your consultation form, and avoid treating anyone at risk. Remember that you should use an extractor fan or ensure good ventilation for all treatments.

❑ Folliculitis is an infection in one or more hair follicles, usually caused by bacteria; the tanning solution may cause further irritation to this condition.

❑ Rosacea is a skin disorder. It causes chronic redness of the face. It can also cause swelling, tiny pimples, and visible broken blood vessels. Rosacea usually affects the cheeks, forehead, chin, and nose, but the ears, chest, and back may also be affected. More than half of people with rosacea also have mild eye symptoms, including redness, burning, and watering. Most people who have this condition have quite sensitive skin. Spray tanning solution **may** irritate this condition. Suggest a patch test.

❑ If spray tanning solution gets into the eyes, irrigate with water for five minutes and if needed seek medical advice.

❑ Avoid spraying direct into eyes, mouth or other mucous membranes (see below).

- Government departments around the EU, USA, Canada and Australia have all approved the products used in spray tanning. The Therapeutic Goods Administration (TGA) is a unit of the Australian Government Department of Health and Ageing and is responsible for administering the provisions of the Therapeutic Goods Act 1989. The TGA carries out a range of assessment and monitoring activities to ensure therapeutic goods available in Australia are of an acceptable standard.

- The Food and Drug Administration (FDA), the Canadian Health Ministry and most of the EU member nations have approved DHA for cosmetic use. It is considered non-toxic and not carcinogenic.

- DHA-based sunless tanning has been recommended by the Skin Cancer Organization, American Academy of Dermatology, Canadian Dermatology Association, The American Cancer Society and the American Medical Association.

- DHA is Food and Drug Administration (FDA) approved for external application but is not deemed safe for application to lips, mucous membranes or if inhaled. This does not mean it is poisonous, it simply means that testing has not established what effects it has other than on the skin. So make sure not to let the spray tan solution get inside the mouth or genital area, eyes or inside the nose. The FDA recommends wearing protective eye goggles and even nose plugs.

Some skin diseases you may benefit from studying

Please do your homework on the following skin diseases and conditions. Without being able to recognise, identify and take precautions against certain conditions you risk your client's health and your own.

- ❑ Eczema: where skin is intact, or when it's broken

- ❑ Psoriasis

- ❑ Ringworm: contagious

- ❑ Impetigo: contagious. There are multiple forms, so research is key

- ❑ Warts: contagious. There are many forms, so research again is vital

- ❑ Vitiligo

- ❑ Verrucas: contagious

- ❑ Herpes: contagious

- ❑ Scabies: contagious

- ❑ Folliculitis: contagious

- ❑ Dermatitis herpetiformis

- ❑ Fungal jock itch: contagious

- ❑ Shingles rash: contagious

- ❑ Hives

- ❑ Rosacea

- ❑ Athlete's foot: contagious

- ❑ Open acne

- ❑ Burns

- ❑ Boils: contagious

- ❑ Rashes: some are contagious, eg most viral rashes. Research is vital

- ❑ Open wounds, cuts and abrasions: should be covered in order to administer spray tan.

The first and simplest place to begin your research into skin conditions is of course the internet, and specifically Google Images. The NHS Direct site, www.nhsdirect.nhs.uk, will provide further depth of knowledge.

19

Promoting and marketing your business

Following the successful completion of a spray tanning course, you need to establish how you're going to publicise your services to potential clients. You'll be itching to start earning, but you need to take your time and think carefully about what you are going to do with your business.

The importance of marketing shouldn't be underestimated, and it requires careful planning. In fact, while I'm on the subject, planning is vital in itself: it helps you think about special occasions and festive seasons that you can use to market your services; and it helps you to budget for those times too. No matter how you go about advertising and marketing your business, always ask your clients how they found you; it'll help you track which avenues work best for you.

Your first big step is to choose your business name. It should be meaningful and memorable, but that doesn't mean it can't be simple. Initially you may not have the budget to have the most beautiful logos and designs made up, so again aim for simplicity and a clean, uncluttered style. Don't rush this; you'll need to produce business cards and leaflets for the most basic level of marketing, so be sure you've considered every detail. Ideally you should get your logo professionally designed, but if your budget is really tight, search your circle of friends for someone in the design industry and cut a deal, or get on the internet. There are various websites and software packages available which will allow you to create your own designs. One site currently free to use is www.cooltext.com, but there are many, many more, so do investigate thoroughly.

Once you've had your cards printed, make sure you always have them with you. Keep some in your handbag, pocket and car, as you never know when you'll meet a potential contact or client.

With any business the best form of advertising is word of mouth. Every client that you treat is a walking advertisement – good or bad. In my experience, no amount of newspaper advertising can compete with the power of recommendations from satisfied clients. When moving to a new area, for instance, a potential client doesn't always look in the newspaper to find a service they require, but may also ask new neighbours, friend, or even someone they've met in a local shop. Bear this in mind before spending lots of money on advertising in the local newspaper and magazines; it may be worth your while distributing your cards or leaflets to local shops, beauty salons, schools and neighbours as a first step.

Of course to generate good word of mouth you need to make the right impression. The quality of your customer service should always be of the highest standard. Always act professionally; dress appropriately, perhaps with a uniform and name badge; be polite, helpful and positive; pay close attention to personal hygiene – and no overpowering perfumes. Care about your clients – they deserve it. They'll repay you by returning time and time again, and by spreading the word.

Try to be the very best at your job. Always be on the lookout for ways in which you could improve your services. Never stop learning, especially if you have lots of competition. You can never learn enough and taking the time to keep up to date with your industry stops clients looking elsewhere. Trade shows are excellent for learning new techniques and finding new products, many of which are given away or offered at a discounted price.

However high you aim to make your service, you may still receive a complaint. In which case be as helpful as possible, and thank the complainant for bringing the matter to your attention. When listening to the complaint always refer to your annotated consultation form and try to resolve the problem quickly. It's sometimes better to ask what they expected from the service than to try to tell them what's happened. Everyone comes across a client that you just can't seem to please and most of the time you know as soon as you meet them. That said, always try to put the problem right, even if it means another spray tan has to be applied. Sometimes it's in everyone's best interest to refund and ask them to take their business elsewhere, but make sure you do it calmly and politely – the faster you resolve the issue, the less likely that customer is to give you bad press.

Build up a local presence

You probably already know lots of people who could help you get started. Try these examples:

- Talk to businesses whose services complement your own. Hairdressers, whether mobile or salon-based, are a prime example, and would probably be happy to give your leaflets to their clients. A salon-based hairdresser may even have some spare space that you may be able to use on a profit-share or rent basis. Depending on the room available you could be based there part-time or even share it with a friend in a related industry. Likewise, sports and leisure centres may have rooms available to rent or on a profit-share basis.

- Approach any ladies you know who are involved in networking, marketing or party planning. They'll be in contact with lots of people who may be interested in your services.

- Many groups, such as women's institutes, local playgroups and nurseries, are always looking to raise extra money, so you may find them receptive to stocking your cards.

- Ask your local health shop if you can leave leaflets or cards on the counter.

- Friends and family working in large companies often have access to a staff notice board or company intranet.

Newspaper advertising

Many local newspapers have health and beauty columns; these may be worth considering when you start up your business. The response tends to be better when your ad is displayed in the main run of the paper - at the front with the editorial. Classified adverts should be chosen with care as they can often lead to unwanted phone calls. There's usually no difference in price structure for these two types of advert. Be wary of being enticed to run consecutive adverts at a reduced rate; it's always worth seeing if an advert gets a worthwhile response before paying out for multiple adverts.

Always consider the location of your ad. If you're being offered cheap space in the gardening section, it's hardly going to drive custom your way. At times newspapers will give free editorial with an advert and that's an option that's always worth exploring – but check and check again for errors. Offers and discounts always catch a reader's eye; a popular means of encouraging clients and tracking the success of an ad at the same time is to offer a discount when a client presents the advert on their appointment day.

More in-depth marketing and promoting

I've been airbrush tanning since 2001 and spent the first three years experimenting with marketing my services. Here's a list of ideas that have worked well enough to keep me growing my business over the past ten years. You may find it helpful as you go through to tick the boxes so you can record which you have tried.

General marketing tips

- ❑ Make sure all your marketing material points out that you're a qualified tanning technician, and display your certificates in your salon.

- ❑ Invest in some business cards that double up as loyalty cards. You can advertise your services and at the same time give your customers a great reason to keep coming back to you by stamping their loyalty card. Once the client has a full card of stamps, they receive a free tan.

- ❑ Display posters in your shop window, for instance 'five for the price of four' prom or school dance tans. There are an awful lot of schoolgirls using sunbeds to prepare for these events, and a spray tan is a far safer option.

- ❑ Offer gift vouchers that your clients can buy for family and friends. If you print them yourself, make sure you number them and record the customer's name and date of purchase to prevent the possibility of being conned.

- ❑ Give out free gifts. This is most effective for clients working in busy offices and factories, where a coffee mug displaying your details, for instance, will get great exposure. There are loads of suppliers out there, but I found that www.vistaprint.co.uk was cost-effective and allows you to save designs for future use.

- ❑ Offer an incentive to new customers, such as a free tan for every five **new** customers they put your way. Keep a record of this on the consultation form or a separate card.

- ❑ Charity spray tans can work well; organising an event and donating 50% of takings to a local charity may even provide enough interest for the local papers or radio to give you coverage.

- ❑ Donate a spray tan or another of your services as a prize in a competition. You could even run your own competition.

- ❑ Record every client's birthday so you can send out birthday cards or emails a week or so beforehand, offering a special price for a tan or even a small free gift at their next booking.

- ❑ Distribute leaflets at local keep-fit and dance classes; join in if you have to.

❑ If you run a salon, consider advertising home visits as well. Some people prefer to book through a salon, especially for special occasions as they perceive it as being more trustworthy, yet still want the convenience of a tan at home.

❑ How many times do you get stuck in traffic and find yourself staring at the back of the car in front of you? If you drive a 4X4 with the spare wheel on the back, consider investing in a custom cover to advertise your business. Alternatively you could have stickers made up for the rear window, the boot lid or the sides of your vehicle. You can get letters that stick on and peel off, and even have magnetic signs made up. I recommend www.platinum-place.co.uk. Consider getting additional stickers made up for friends and family to display.

❑ Weddings are a prime target market for spray tan technicians. Consider attending wedding exhibitions and leaving your details with exhibitors. You might even persuade stall-holders to display your information, especially if you can offer an incentive. Depending on costs, you may even feel it worthwhile exhibiting for yourself.

❑ Tanning parties are fun and the profits are quite high. Supplying a couple of bottles of wine and a good CD adds to the fun atmosphere, and it's always a good idea to offer the host a free spray tan. You may want to turn your tanning tent away from the seating area, or use a separate room. Be prepared though: as more clients get tanned, they do seem to get braver and end up wanting their bottoms and chests tanned. Great for mobile technicians, but with the right preparation in place you could offer tanning parties at a salon too.

❑ If you are really brave and confident you could go into a shopping centre with a clipboard and pick out shoppers that look like they could become potential clients. Tell them you're looking for 10 models to spray tan free. Just give a business card to those that say no, and book in those who accept, hand them 20 or so business cards with the promise of another free tan for every five people she refers.

❑ If you set up as a product reseller, visit your local salons and leave sample bottles for the staff to try. Leave your contact business card and details of an introductory offer on their first order.

❑ Try to keep your marketing ideas to yourself until you're using them. Information has a funny way of finding its way to competitors, so don't even tell your friends – especially if they're in the same line of work!

More marketing in your local area

Most of your potential customers will live or work locally, so it makes sense to raise awareness in your community and nearby towns and villages. Start close to home and work your way outwards to what you consider the maximum distance a customer is likely to travel for a spray tan – probably ten miles. Those of you who are mobile technicians may be prepared to travel further for each customer, so choose your travelling radius accordingly and try to book clients from each particular location into the same day so that you can keep your costs down.

❑ Check out the competition in your area. Keep an eye on their services, prices and promotions. It'll help you gauge your place in the market, and allow you to offer additional services that'll give you that competitive edge.

❑ Have two versions of the same leaflet – one on high grade paper, the other on cheaper paper. You'll keep the high-end leaflets for more upmarket marketing ideas, and use the lower grade leaflets for mass marketing.

❑ Search out businesses which might be prepared to display your business cards or leaflets, even if only in exchange for you offering to do the same for them. You'll have the greatest chance of success with complementary businesses such as hairdressers, but you'd be surprised at who'll agree to help. If you're leaving leaflets, choose the quality that matches the business. A wedding venue for instance should receive the best quality marketing material. Track how many long it takes each business to run out of your leaflets so that when you restock, you deliver no more than needed.

Approach local:

❑ Hairdressers and beauty salons

❑ Leisure centres (where all sorts of competitions may be held)

❑ Sports and fitness centres

❑ Hotels

❑ Wedding and reception venues

❑ Wedding and formal wear shops, including lingerie

- Photographers' studios

- Modelling and casting agencies

- Fancy dress shops and party-related shops

- Florists, including florist wholesalers

- Dental and doctors' surgeries

- Coffee shops

- Dance schools and ice rinks, including adult classes

Target other local businesses; the obvious and the not so obvious:

- Local supermarket and shop display boards – if they're positioned in line with the checkout queues, so much the better!

- Adult, belly and pole dancing classes

- Post Office notice boards. The Post Office TV channel if you have a larger budget!

- Sandwich vans – for the delivery staff to distribute

- Retirement homes (it's the staff you'll be targeting for tans, but residents may be interested in other treatments you provide)

- Paperboys and girls. Cut out the middleman and offer cash to the messenger

- Strippers (only for the brave, as you'll most likely be confronted with full nudity)

- Senior schools. Best targeted in prom season, and best approached in person around four weeks before any given event. Push the health benefits of avoiding sun exposure; an important lesson for kids

- Junior schools and nurseries. Parents spend a lot of time waiting around…

- ❑ School fetes – whether to provide discounted on-the-spot partial tans, simply distribute leaflets or set up a stall

Give people an incentive to display your marketing material, or an incentive to buy:

- ❑ Offer a free tan for every five clients recommended directly to you, or for group bookings

- ❑ A free tan in return for displaying your marketing material

- ❑ A free tan for brides who get their bridesmaids booked in

- ❑ Offer a free tan to brides a month before the wedding. They'll be back...

- ❑ Offer a free tan to the organiser who brings five customers to your salon at once, or the host who books five tans at a home location. Alternatively, make this a 'five tans for the price of four' offer. This sort of offer goes down extremely well with teenagers, so consider using it on school prom-oriented flyers and posters

- ❑ Reciprocate by displaying other businesses' cards and posters

I've given away a lot of free tans over the years; it's an extremely effective tool which generates a lot of repeat business if your workmanship is good. When you're using the precision airbrush gun system it's not an expensive exercise to give away free tans. If you were to target a factory at lunchtime you might get to tan ten people who'll then be telling their friends and colleagues all about the experience. That kind of word of mouth advertising makes a real impact. I've even picked people off the street fairly randomly, offering them a free tan on condition that they hand out some leaflets to their friends.

Leaving leaflets on car windscreens is a worthwhile mass marketing method. Don't target the car park of a company that's been good enough to display your marketing material inside however. Use your cheaper leaflets for this, since most will of course be thrown away, and British weather can turn at the drop of a hat, ruining your best efforts. If it looks like rain... stay home in the dry.

Target car parks at local:

- ❑ Supermarkets

- ❑ Shopping centres

- ❑ Garden centres

- ❑ Pubs and clubs (do take care if you're doing this at night)

- ❑ Sports and leisure centres

- ❑ Cinemas

- ❑ Car boot sales

- ❑ Schools

- ❑ High street parking and public car parks

- ❑ If you have a larger budget for your advertising, try local radio – choosing a time slot following the news or weather at rush hour if possible.

- ❑ Theme your advertising. Offer promotions during holiday or festive seasons; put up posters highlighting school prom spray tans during the spring and early summer; create health-promoting leaflets highlighting skin cancer awareness for doctors' surgeries; watch the local paper for modelling/ice skating/dancing competitions where entrants will appreciate a tanned physique. Get creative.

Online marketing – using the internet

- ❑ The easiest and cheapest way to establish an online presence is to use social media. Your first port of call should be www.facebook.com. There you can set up a Facebook business page, provided you already have a personal profile. From there on you can get your friends to publicise your business on your behalf, and raise awareness in your local area. www.twitter.com is a very different social networking tool, and it's not for everyone. But take the time to dip in and see how it works. It might just appeal to you, and it can be a great way to generate new business. The third most important networking website is www.linkedin.com. This is different altogether; it's a business networking website. Connect with people you know professionally, and ask business-related questions in the dedicated areas. These websites, along with many more social networking sites, offer tremendous marketing potential. They can take a lot of effort, but they can be a great deal of fun. There are lots of comprehensive guides to how to use these websites to your best advantage (just go to www.google.co.uk and start searching!), but for a brief overview you might want to download this free guide to marketing your business online: http://www.ahcopy.co.uk/Ten-steps-to-being-found-online.pdf. It's an easy step-by-step introduction to helping people to find your website.

❑ The next step is to set up a website. Initially you may want to do this cheaply, rather than paying for a professional web designer. If so, there are several places you can go with free website design templates – all you'll need to do is think about the structure of your website and enter your text and images. Perhaps the best starting point is Google's GBBO (Getting British Business Online) initiative: www.gbbo.co.uk. As I write this, in the summer of 2010, the site is offering free websites to new businesses. It's completely free for two years and then, should you wish to carry on, the annual charge is the most affordable marketing you can do. The sites aren't too complicated to design, but before you begin do make sure you've got your words worked out, and save your work as you go along.

❑ When you create your website try not to include **too** much information on the before-care, aftercare and exfoliating sections, simply because discussing these details should form part of your personal relationship with clients. You can never afford to assume that a client has read and absorbed all the necessary information just because it's on your website. That said, your website **should** demonstrate to potential clients that you know your business, and you care about the results.

❑ If you really want a professional design for your website and indeed business cards, leaflets and other marketing material, then search out a reputable designer with a great portfolio of work. I can personally recommend Ian Hutchins. He designed the book cover for *Walking in Sunshine* and nothing was too much trouble. He was very professional, reasonably priced and helped me enter the world of the unknown! You can find Ian at www.hutchinscreative.co.uk; have a look at some of his award-winning work online.

❏ Submit your website to all the major search engines. If you use a web designer he or she may provide this service. As a starting point, make sure your business is listed on Google Maps: www.google.com/local/add/businesscenter.

❏ One of the most important ways to help people find your website is to get it listed in online directories. These come in various categories:

• Business directories, eg www.yell.com, www.thomsonlocal.com, www. business-directory-uk.co.uk. Some, such as Yell and Thomson Local, are free, others have a cost associated. Go with the free directories first, then consider any paid directories on a case by case basis

• Specialist directories, eg www.directorybeauty.com and www.beautyfinder. co.uk. Beauty Finder currently offers a 15% discount on business advertising packages when you enter the promotional code SUNSHINE when adding your business.

• Local directories. Search Google for websites related to your town and county. Many will have free business directories where you can list your services

❏ You can even design a website toolbar, which you can send to your clients and friends. This keeps your site to the forefront of their mind every time they use the internet. www.ourtoolbar.com provides this service for free. As with any service you use, whether paid or free, check the terms and conditions thoroughly.

Diversifying

Being able to provide more than just the precision airbrush spray tan service can give you a distinct competitive advantage. If you've got all the airbrush tanning equipment you might want to consider training in some related disciplines. Make sure any training you undertake or courses you attend result in a certificate that your insurer will accept.

❏ False nails are a great finishing touch for a special occasion or party. I even do kids' nails, a service that's in demand with young bridesmaids and girls going to the school prom. These are as simple as white tips cut and filed to fit, with a couple of coats of clear gloss nail varnish. They only take half an hour, so you can keep your prices low. Youngsters generally love to tell everyone they've had their nails done, so this is a fantastic way of generating word-of-mouth publicity.

- ❑ Offer airbrush nail art for free if clients have the gel or acrylic nails done. Everyone loves getting something for nothing and it makes your service different from others. You'll need to change your needle and pot for nail art, and depending on its type, perhaps the gun itself; the spray tanning system (compressor) stays the same.

- ❑ I also offer airbrush make-up, which is fantastic for brides, bridesmaids, mother of the bride, proms and other special occasions. It lasts all day, looks amazing, and you can achieve a great range of different looks – from soft and natural to striking. If a client has bad skin tone, you can camouflage almost everything yet give the impression of having no make-up on at all.

- ❑ TV make-up and professional photo shoots often use airbrush make-up these days. The high definition digital cameras pick up miniscule flaws, and the airbrush technique is most effective at disguising them. Finding a good course can be a problem, so attend beauty shows and watch the seminars. That way you can assess the tutor at work.

- ❑ Do your research on what your competitors are charging for all their services. Make sure your prices are good, no matter how good you are. Adding a free treatment that will complement the airbrush make-up will usually make your service stand out from the competition.

- ❑ Airbrush tattoos go down a treat at school fetes. Queues for children's tattoos usually go round the school hall. I only charge £1 to £3 for each, depending on size. Stick to black ink though (which costs around £8 per bottle), as you won't have time to clean the airbrush between colours. You can buy books of stencils online, providing the ever-popular hearts, dragons, Chinese writing and tribal symbols.

- ❑ If you're going to provide both partial tans and tattoos at the one fete, make sure your compressor is up to the continuous work and that you have two airbrushes set up – nobody wants black ink in their new tan…

- ❑ Make sure you pay the school's table fee, rather than a share of your profits – unless you're raising money for the school of course. If you've got children at the school, send them in the week before the event sporting their own tattoos – excellent publicity that will get all the kids talking.

❑ Likewise, providing airbrush tattoos at children's parties can be a long-term money spinner. You won't make a great deal from the event itself as the parent organising it is unlikely to have a vast budget, but you **can** make sure that one of your tanning leaflets is put in every party bag along with the tattoo aftercare leaflets.

❑ Of course you can also provide airbrush tattoos from your salon, or even come to arrangements with local nightclubs. If you do want to tap into that market, make sure you use your consultation forms, take payment before applying the tattoo, and that your working night finishes by 1am at the latest – any later and you're dealing with people who are just too drunk. If you're not keen on working in a noisy club environment find out whether you can leave cards or leaflets at the cloakroom, toilets or on tables.

❑ I suspect airbrush tattooing courses are all very similar, but make sure your chosen course provides a recognised certificate and that your insurance company will insure you. Again, you always need a consultation form, and parental permission for under-18s. Be organised – have your forms set up so that if you've generated a queue your customers can be filling out and signing their forms as they wait. Be prepared for lots of missing pens! If you're airbrushing at a children's party, have your forms sent out to the guests in advance. It'll save you a lot of time and gives parents the chance to opt out early.

❑ Offer a free airbrush tattoo to girls having prom spray tans; they'll certainly tell their friends.

❑ If you are already a hairdresser you've got the perfect diversity of service ready and waiting. You should be offering a combination of services for all the usual special occasions.

❑ But you don't need to be a hairdresser to learn hair styling for special occasions. If you decide to offer hair styling you need to be completely clear that you are not a hairdresser, and that **you do not cut hair**. Make sure that the course you attend will give you an insurance certificate. It's quite easy to just learn styling the hair; www.youtube.com, for instance, has plenty of video tutorials, but you really do need to master your techniques and styles – you're contributing to someone's **very** special day after all. Build up your own portfolio to show off your work.

- Facials, massage and Indian head massage are popular with brides on the eve or morning of their big day.

- Manicures work for any occasion.

- Pedicures are particularly popular with weddings and proms, as open-toe shoes are often worn.

- Waxing is also very popular but as I've mentioned before, you need to make sure you perform this service a few days **before** their tan, as skin may be sensitive to the process.

- Professional semi-permanent eyelash extensions are very popular and are fantastic for any occasion. Again, check for a reputable trainer.

- Eyelash perming and tinting as well as eyebrow shaping are excellent services to complement your existing offerings.

- Body wraps prove popular when people are hoping to shed an inch or so before an important event.

20
Sampling spray tanning solutions

So many students and customers ask me to recommend tanning solutions and this I've found very difficult to do as there are so many on the market.

What's more, when we want to try a different solution we usually have to buy quite large bottles. If we don't like it, the solution goes to waste.

After a bit of thought I decided to email selected spray tanning companies all over the world to find those who'd provide sample bottles for free or for shipping costs alone. The response was fantastic, and I've included a directory of providers at the end of this section. Some will even refund the costs against a first order, and others offer substantial discounts to new customers.

Obtaining free samples is a perfect opportunity to gain broader experience with the different solutions available, and will help you to decide which you prefer and work out the best possible product price.

Please don't abuse any free sample offers though. The companies I'm recommending have supplied an outstanding service and their willingness to supply free products is a show of trust, as well as a sign that they're confident in their products and recognise that technicians need to make up their own minds which products to use.

Giving out free or discounted samples is a significant cost for the suppliers to absorb, so if you do get sent a sample from a company, please be helpful and respectful when they then request feedback.

As ever, you should always test a product several times on yourself or someone whose skin you know very well, before you try it on a paying client. Taking time over decisions now will save you money in the future.

I'd also be grateful when you contact these companies if you could let them know you found their details in *Walking in Sunshine*, since I've been in touch with them all.

Some have given dedicated email contacts for Walking in Sunshine readers, some have applied codes, and some have recommended contact via their website, but this list is up to date as of August 2010. It's worth checking all company website details though before you take the trouble of emailing, as a few months can see a lot of change in industry! A phone call is often even better as you could find out about even more offers.

This is a fantastic opportunity to try new products from different companies and even different countries. Being able to boast that your solutions are from America or Australia may just get you noticed, and organic, natural and anti-aging solutions also tend to draw attention. Perhaps you could run a special offer for a couple of weeks to introduce a new spray tanning solution and see if your clients prefer it. People like choice, and this will broaden your appeal.

Thank you to all the companies that have supplied their details. You all took the time to talk with me, and I'm so pleased you recognise that spray tanning technicians welcome guidance and will benefit from trial sized bottles. I hope your accommodating approach brings you plenty of new customers.

Good luck to all the technicians in trying these solutions – I hope you find a fantastic selection to offer your clients.

Specialist directory

WEBSITE	EMAIL	PERSO
www.suntana.com	sales@suntana.com	
www.freshindulgence.co.uk Quote code Fresh: will deduct postage cost on first order if sample liked, as well as a 15% discount.	info@freshindulgence.co.uk	Catherir
www.latanning.co.uk Quote code stu/disc. Discount voucher available if solution sample is liked.	info@latanning.co.uk	
www.fantasytan.co.uk Contact for further information on offers.	markrestrick@rjmhairandbeauty.com	Mark
www.beaubronz.co.uk New customers: 30% discount on first order if sample is liked.	info@beaubronz.co.uk Straight from website	Abi
www.whitetobrown.com Often have offers available.	sales@whitetobrown.com	Gemma
www.aspire2pure.co.uk Quote code walking in sunshine and receive 10% discount on first order of over £100 if sample is liked.	info@aspire2pure.co.uk	Susie
www.spraytan.com	ashamax@gmail.com	Brian
www.unitedbeauty.co.uk Many promotions for new customers.	emcshefferty@unitedbeauty.co.uk	Elaine
www.thesunlessstore.com	admin@thevanitygirl.com	Kevin & Debb
www.risingstarbeauty.com	info@risingstarbeauty.com	
www.celebritysecretstanning.co.uk	info@celebritysecretstanning.co.uk	Sam
www.sjolietanning.com	Straight from website	
www.unreal.me.uk Costs for sample refunded on first order if sample liked.	liz@unreal.me.uk	Liz
www.tampabaytan.com	Straight from website or help@tampabaytan.com	Leah
www.abcbeautyltd.co.uk Introductory offer: VAT-free on opening orders if sample liked.	info@abcbeautyltd.co.uk	
www.australianorganicspraytansupplies.com.au	organicspraytan@gmail.com	Danielle
www.roxtan.com.au Quote code ROX769	sales@roxtan.com.au	Ryan M
www.sunfx.com.au	info@sunfx.com.au	Daniel c Emma

SOLUTION	COST	COUNTRY
Suntana Solution	Free sample. Cost of shipping within UK	UK
Fresh indulgence Solution Anti-Aging Solutions 100% Vegan	Free sample. Cost for shipping within UK	UK
LA Tanning Company	Free sample & free shipping within UK	UK
Fantasy Tan Solution	Free sample. Cost of shipping within UK	Northern Ireland UK
Beau Bronz Solutions	Free sample & free shipping within UK	UK
White to Brown Solution	Free sample & free shipping within UK	UK
Pure Solution	Free sample & free shipping within UK	UK
Different Solutions	Free sample. Cost of shipping within UK Free sample & shipping to USA	USA
Solglo Solution	Free sample. Free shipping within UK	UK
Different Solutions	Free sample. Cost of shipping within UK Free solution & shipping to USA	USA
A,C,E Solutions	Free sample. Cost of shipping within UK	Ireland
Celebrity Secrets Solutions	Free sample. Cost of shipping within UK	UK
Sjolie Tanning Solution	Free sample. Cost of shipping within UK Free sample & free shipping to USA	USA
Unreal Solutions	Cost for sample & cost of shipping within UK	UK
TanEnvy Solutions Sample pack	Cost for sample Cost of shipping within UK	USA
Tropical Sun Solutions	Cost for sample Free shipping within UK	UK
Natural & Organic Solution	Not available to UK Free sample & shipping within Australia	Australia
Rox Tan	Free sample. Cost for shipping within Australia	Australia
SunFX	Free sample free shipping within Australia	Australia

Your enquiry, whether by phone or email, might run along these lines:

I'm a spray tanning technician looking for new products to offer my clients. I recently bought Sam Whitehead's book *Walking in Sunshine* from Castlepoint Tanning and found your contact details in the specialist directory.

I'm interested in trying your tanning solution, preferably in a sample size. Would it be possible to send me a sample or trial-sized bottle of (insert product name and the tan tone percentage you'd like to sample)?

I'd also be grateful if you could include any relevant product information, samples and prices.

Many thanks,

Don't forget to provide your name, address and contact details!

21
Good luck!

I really hope this book sets you on the path to a successful career and provides you with the confidence to be every bit as good as you can be.

Take care

Sam

Walking in Sunshine...
every day is beautiful as long as you can see it.

New College Nottingham
Learning Centres

Disclaimer

The information and data published in the book is strictly for informational purposes. Any opinions or viewpoints presented in this book are those of the contributing author and do not necessarily represent the philosophy or viewpoints of the beauty industry as a whole.

Professionals have not reviewed the information contained in this book with the knowledge required to validate that the data is accurate, complete, or reliable.

The author accepts no liability for the content of this book, or for the consequences of any actions taken on the basis of the information provided, unless that information is subsequently confirmed in writing.